To Sana,
Congrats on all your success. Keep inspiring me!

6/4/19

That's What Friends Are For
On the Women Who Inspired Me

Patrick L. Riley

Dorpie
DORPIE BOOKS • WASHINGTON

DORPIE BOOKS
WASHINGTON

www.dorpiebooks.com

Copyright © 2018 by Patrick L. Riley

Some of this work appeared on my blog, *The Life of Riley*.

Author photograph © by Frank Ishman

All photos are from the personal archives of Patrick L. Riley.

All rights reserved, including right of reproduction in whole or in part, in any form.

ISBN: 978-0-9996794-0-1

Contents

Introduction 1
Chapter 1 - Oprah Winfrey's Legends Ball 9
Chapter 2 - Visionaries 21
Chapter 3 - Miss Ross and Other Gay Icons 35
Chapter 4 - Angels 55
Chapter 5 - Women on Broadway 75
Chapter 6 - Black Beauties 97
Chapter 7 - Famous Families 111
Chapter 8 - Talk Show Hosts 133
Chapter 9 - Television and Movie Star 145
Chapter 10 - Reality Stars 189
Chapter 11 - The (Gay) Family 207
Chapter 12 - Singers 221
Chapter 13 - The Creatives 259
Chapter 14 - Journalists 271
Chapter 15 - Women of Hip Hop 287
Chapter 16 - All-Star Karaoke 299
Acknowledgements 314

This book is dedicated to the E Wing Crew and they know who they are. Though I've not known them for a lifetime, I sometimes feel my life began when I met these particular peers. From our beginning, they observed my obsession with divas was more than a dalliance. Instead, they joined my daily celebration. If just tolerated. Now, we are settled into our adulthood selves and my dream girls continue to dazzle me, still daily. Now though, they have become my interview subjects, project clients, bosses, buddies, mentors and more. Through it all, my people from childhood remain on the ride—encouraging, loving, and lifting me up as I shoot this love letter out to my galaxy of stars. Inspiring me. The best friends. Forever.

Introduction

I've been blessed to work in the media business for twenty-five years. I started out in 1992 as a news reporter trainee and a local morning show producer in Atlanta. My move to New York City in 1995 would give me access to a larger playing field, first handling duties for Geraldo Rivera whose primetime show *Rivera Live*, I produced.

But perhaps I'm best known as having been a freelance field producer for *The Oprah Winfrey Show* for over thirteen years. Some would call that a career highlight, given my assignments dispatched me front and center to interview the world's notables. One day the focus of my attention could be President Bill Clinton at the White House's Roosevelt Room on Martin Luther King Jr.'s birthday in 2001. On another day, in May of 2005, it was Senator Barack Obama as he and his wife Michelle attended Oprah's historic Legends Ball, where she honored a host of African-American legends in front of an esteemed room of entertainers, politicians and tastemakers. "It's never hard for me to extol the wonders and beauty of black women." Said the future president of the United States. I've felt the very same way about black women in arts and entertainment practically from in the womb.

Though a Southern boy since I was nine years old, born to two Savannah, Georgia natives, my Air Force-enlisted dad made a global family out of me and my older siblings Janice and Herman. We lived in places like Berlin and Tokyo for years before calling Valdosta, Georgia home. I came into my memories around this time and I knew I was a bit different than other boys. Though, as young as I was, I didn't think to call the feeling "being gay." What I do know is that I loved to spend time with my mom and my sister as they watched their "stories," more popularly known as soap operas.

And when it came to culture and the arts, I was usually mom's automatic date to go to the Savannah Civic Center to catch the symphony orchestra or whichever *Nutcracker* came to town. Not Dad, not my siblings, but me. My mother also spent a lot of dedicated time with me on my speeches, school play lines and costumes for special performances or recitals.

While I enjoyed these activities, adults also yelled at me to stop acting like a "sissy," signaling a concern that my behavior, that threatening hint of effeminacy, might not be fully accepted as I grew older. Given that I was sensitive about this and wanted to fit in, I began to deprogram some of what was natural to me. I took on as many socially acceptable forms of behavior that I could. As my siblings believed I needed to get my head out of the books and get outside to play ball, I participated in little league football and sixth grade basketball on the military base until my childhood asthma kicked in. Though I did snag a tackle or two as a center for the Southside Raiders, I couldn't continue to play with them because the games were on Thursdays. Our VCR was down, and I was not going to miss one more *Gimme a Break* episode starring one of my favorites from the time, Nell Carter.

Nonetheless, I did have amazing male buddies who were ride or die regardless of my being perceived as gay or effeminate. They gave me support when I was unsure about how to feel comfortable in my own skin. I was a little boy who may not have had much interest in basketball or football, but I did like to ride my bike, bowl and play video games. Contrary to stereotypes, I've always hated to shop so my beloved mother and I didn't bond on that front as many gay sons do with their mothers. However, on any given day, you could see me channeling my inner Debbie Allen or Leroy from *Fame* throughout the house.

I was captivated by what I saw on the screen, believing my unconditional-to-the-core friends were on the television and in entertainment magazines. I connected to these friends differently as they seemed to speak my language. My father says my passion for female entertainers and divas goes back to when he'd take me to the library and I'd routinely borrow books on the likes of Diahann Carroll, Ruby Dee or Lena Horne.

I've always been fascinated with Hollywood ever since I first heard of it. If my mother snagged a *National Enquirer* because some headline grabbed her attention, or if she was working part-time and wanted to be updated on her CBS daytime stories and picked up a *Soap Opera Digest*, I always enjoyed them as bonus reading after my studies. I was the master of *TV Guide*, reviewing and highlighting next week's programming for family viewing and, before VCRs, coordinating who would watch what and where they would watch it when schedules conflicted. Inside the pages of those magazines, in the frame of that box called a TV, wherever pop culture seduced its way into my life, I was hooked.

Women in arts and entertainment were the muses from my childhood who made me feel better when I was an unsure little boy who didn't quite know how to live in his own truth. These women could tear my heart out with a melody or a soliloquy in a movie, appealing to the outcast I sometimes felt like in my search for acceptance.

By high school, I had the jaded notion that there was a hard road ahead and that maybe I wouldn't be able to handle it. I wondered if I would ever come out as a gay man, as reconciling my insides to what was going on outside was difficult. Would I continue to go the course that society wanted me to? Could I marry a woman? These were big questions I had to start asking myself while peers were taking the next steps into their intimate relationships.

Years later, having made it to college, I got to keep such concerns at bay in a swim of overcompensation and endless activities. I let my ambitions fly by taking extra classes at Clark Atlanta University while securing my liberal arts requirements at Morehouse. It was a lot to handle but I juggled it all, got it done and graduated in four years. Many classmates have shared that you could always see me quickly walking through campus to get to and coming from a litany of appointments. What they don't know was the voices of my favorite ladies were playing in my head, inspiring me to keep going as I gradually became more comfortable with my sexual orientation and came out to others.

There was a legion of live or onscreen moments that shaped who I am. When the concert special *Sisters in the Name of Love* aired on HBO on July 12, 1986, I was blown away at the diva-powered hour. The spectacular evening was recorded before a live audience at the historic Aquarius Theater in Hollywood and included performances of fifteen soul, gospel and pop classics.

Gladys Knight welcomed Dionne Warwick and Patti LaBelle to join her onstage for a rendition of the single "That's What Friends Are For." This was Warwick's 1985-86 No. 1 hit that she recorded alongside Gladys, Stevie Wonder and Elton John. The single raised over $3 million for the American Foundation for AIDS research. Written by Burt Bacharach and Carol Bayer Sager, it became 1986's biggest selling single according to *Billboard* and *Cashbox* magazines. Statistically, it's a palpable and perfect example of how the music industry responds when there's a need.

"These two ladies and I have been friends for a very long time," Dionne says near the end of the show. "And the fact is that we will always be friends. Always." I loved seeing these women as sisters, still loving on each other and finding ways to lift each other up as well as lifting the world up. Their example has encouraged so much of how I live my life today and who I will call a true friend. Indeed, this special, and so many more like it have set a tone for me by showing me how to appreciate the friends before me and the people on the screen who have inspired me to be brave, open and free with how I choose to live. They may never know my name, but they bring me joy, love and inspiration when I may not be able to conjure it from anywhere else.

These are special ladies who validated me immensely, and I found myself wanting to know more about them. I wanted to be around them when I could, I wanted to genuinely connect with them and be a cheerleader or promoter for their work. Before I knew it, I was interviewing these celebrity women, producing their projects, helping them promote their initiatives and forwarding their campaigns. It has been my pleasure to do so. After all, that's what friends are for, right?

I take my hat off to each and everyone one of these women. I've had the chance to tell many of them that they inspire me. This book is a love letter to those I haven't told and it's a follow up to those I have. Whether extended time or a stolen moment, there's an energy that comes off of Beyoncé or Janet Jackson when I touch their hand to greet them. More than that, when we can connect inside such a window, we are one-on-one. I share some of those rare anecdotes that demonstrate the love and light these women further represent up close and personal. Standing on the shoulder pads of my favorites is a new crop of women I've been interviewing and meeting over the last decade including Brandy, Monica, Issa Rae, Tamar Braxton and more. In the Instagram era, it's a treat to connect to these ladies who, beyond the emoticons and tweets, show their reverence for their fans and LGBTQ allies. Up close, I've seen women who were born in the '80s and '90s deliver another generation of black girl magic that inspires a new generation of fans. And for those like me, who still keep up, it's a blessing and I salute these women.

Featuring more than twenty years in the business and just over a decade of blogging about pop culture and the positivity that looms around it, *That's What Friends Are For* is part memoir. It is also partly an entertainment diary of a TV producer and personality who has interacted with and interviewed hundreds of my own and the world's favorites. I've taken the time on these pages to wax nostalgic and pop cultural on these women and what they've meant to me along with what they've meant to the universe. I'll take you on the ride of what it felt like to interview so many legends and great female artists under one roof. I breakdown how not only an obsession with Miss Ross, but also all things Motown, would lead me to interview Motown Founder Berry Gordy alongside Diana Ross at the Opening Night of Broadway's *Motown the Musical*. There are many names I'm sure you know that are associated with Motown and its legacy. In addition to reflecting on that roster, I share information about the behind the scenes players who've become household names of their own like songwriter and performer Valerie Simpson.

In addition to Oprah, I have had the opportunity to produce and work alongside other role models of mine in the media business including Wendy Williams. And to have lived a life where I actually thought my generation would never experience another Billie Holliday, I have tales of icons we've lost too soon such as Natalie Cole, Whitney Houston and Vesta.

You'll read stories on more than black women in entertainment as I explore a mix of narratives focusing on businesswomen, authors, journalists, reality stars, stage performers and activists. Each chapter will include a scrapbook that I personally curated including snapshots from my personal collection along with some special memories inside each caption. I am excited to share these photos, two of which include me alongside my childhood idol, Diana Ross. Another shot taken with Beyoncé in Manila is particularly special because she serenaded me with "Happy Birthday" after we took it. Each photo has its own special story.

As we all lead our busy lives, I have seen my social media timelines come alive of late with references to pop culture, nostalgia, throwbacks and flashbacks. We say, "Happy Birthday" to the celebrities as if they are our friends. On Facebook, they are actually called friends. In my head, as long as I can remember, these powerful women have moved me and I'm hoping that they move you too. Writing this project has been a labor of love. So much of what these women have produced and presented to us, serves as a soundtrack or milestone in my life. Taking the time to pull those memories up and shape them into prose wasn't always easy to do but it was therapeutic. I revisited hurts from the past that I thought had healed and was unsure about sharing such vulnerable sentiments to the public. My trust though, is that many readers will be able to relate.

If just one gay kid can find a spot of inspiration in this text along with others who can give support to the LGBTQ community, my efforts will have been worth it. I invite you to walk down memory lane with me. As you read, perhaps I'll jog your own memories about this unofficial sorority of diverse women who have inspired myself as well as so many others.

chapter 1

Oprah Winfrey's Legends Ball

In 2005, to get to Promised Land, the name my boss Oprah Winfrey gave her 65-acre estate in Montecito, California, I took a cab from my home in Ridgefield Park, New Jersey to JFK Airport. Due to the time difference, time seemed to have stood still when five hours later, I landed in Santa Barbara. In every direction I looked, blue skies were abundant and flanked by yellow beaches and gray mountains. Then it was my turn to drive up the winding roads, past one secluded estate after another, before reaching Miss Winfrey's grounds.

By Oprah's design, this Southern California mansion, likely built long after the Civil War, resembled a Southern plantation. As I walked beneath the village of looming live oaks along a cobblestone path named Hallelujah Lane, taking in the benefits of an aromatic breeze created by the nearby pond and formal rose garden, the estates moniker seemed fitting. Surely this oasis was God-endorsed.

This beauty wasn't unfamiliar to me. In truth, some of my childhood was spent in Savannah, Georgia which was considered too beautiful to be burned down during the Civil War. The locale was the focus of my first book, an assignment handed out by my 6th grade teacher Miss Lokey called, "A Child's View of Savannah Squares." My goal at that age was to fit in and not make waves. Which was why I didn't insist that we include extensive details about what went on north of Johnson Square where trades were made for the enslaved, who would provide the free labor for the Wickersham iron works surrounding the grandest homes. The book mentioned the Spanish moss cascading through the woods, but even at that young age I knew there once hung from the trees the strange fruit called, a black man.

My understanding of local history was corroborated through scenes from movies like *Glory* in which the 54th Massachusetts Volunteer Infantry, the first black regiment in the U.S. army, parade along River Street which runs along the south bank of the Savannah River.

Another work that spoke to my understanding of the past was the film adaptation of the book *Midnight in the Garden of Good and Evil*. I have family ties to this Savannah-based story of the decade which was a famed *New York Times* bestseller. While I wouldn't meet the book's Lady Chablis, a transgender woman and local drag queen and entertainer, until I was an affirming adult, my Aunt Tuga had been the maid for the work's central character, Jim Williams. He was tried an unprecedented four times and ultimately acquitted, and "rightfully so" according to my aunt, for the shooting death of assistant Danny Lewis Hansford in Williams Savannah home, Mercer House.

Imagine the mental and spiritual distance I had to travel to wrap my mind around where I'm from and where I was on the day I visited the Promised Land.

All my life, I'd witnessed black women do amazing things from my paternal grandmother Daisy Mae Riley who raised eight great kids, to my mom who as a child contracted rheumatic fever and wasn't expected to live past her eighth birthday. But she survived. This is the plainest fact for most black women despite daunting odds, they survive. But the women who were being honored at Oprah's home that weekend had managed even more than that, much more in fact.

I came to know this in a personal way when I learned Shirley Caesar was one of the honorees. Pastor Shirley Caesar is known as the Mother of Gospel Music, but the ambitions exhibited by this Durham, North Carolina baby girl of twelve kids was felt when she was ten years old. By thirteen, she was called to spread the gospel throughout North Carolina while Jim Crow laws were still in effect.

In the '40's and '50s, restaurants refused to serve her, and she suffered through all types of unfair treatment towards African Americans. Shirley's perseverance and determination took her to North Carolina Central College where she studied business education. She eventually auditioned for Chicago's popular female gospel group, The Caravans, which was looking for a new member. She was immediately hired and left school for a life of singing and ministry. Eventually she tabulated one hundred and fifty concerts per year, did volunteer work for the poor, received numerous Grammy awards and made over thirty albums.

The first diva I ever knew was my mother. She had been the lead-singer of the popular Savannah-based gospel church quartet founded in the '40s, the Georgia Roses. She, like Gospel Hall of Famer Shirley Caesar, would perform extensively along the southern and eastern coasts of the United States, forging an international reputation along the way. But life, choices and chance would lead my mother away from the path Pastor Caesar and these other legendary women traveled.

As field producer, I'd been chosen by Ms. Winfrey to interview all of the women attendees taking part in the three-day weekend. The goal was to simply be a fly on the wall and capture the evening for archival purposes and amidst that, the mission was to get quick soundbites from each of the honorees and guests throughout the weekend. My work would eventually be used as footage for a future ABC primetime special.

Many of the women I'd admired as a child were now springing to life from the pages of glossies, television screens, and on rare occasions, the stage. Imagine your job is to ask them the questions you've always wanted to ask. Such a feat wasn't anything I had to imagine as it was my reality.

Diahann Carroll, who had spent residential time in Santa Barbara as black folks' Civil Rights were still being wrangled, told me a year or so after the occasion that she wouldn't have expected to see a black woman host this many black women at a black-owned estate.

Here's ABC's press release describing the work we did that weekend:

OPRAH WINFREY BRINGS A PERSONAL DREAM TO LIFE AS SHE HONORS 25 LEGENDARY WOMEN IN OPRAH WINFREY'S LEGENDS BALL, MONDAY, MAY 22 ON THE ABC TELEVISION NETWORK

As the one-year anniversary of her memorable Legends Ball nears, Oprah Winfrey brings to television her personal archival footage from the three-day, once-in-a-lifetime celebration honoring 25 legendary women in the fields of art, entertainment and civil rights. "These women, who have been meaningful to so many of us over the years, are legends who have been magnificent in their pioneering and advancing of African American women. It is because of their steps that our journey has no boundaries." Said Oprah Winfrey.

This historic celebration included an unforgettable luncheon which was a glamorous white-tie ball and a heart-bursting gospel brunch. In this one-hour special, Oprah shares her memories, candid celebrity interviews and intimate behind-the-scenes moments from this event.

The 25 legendary women celebrated include Maya Angelou, Shirley Caesar, Diahann Carroll, Elizabeth Catlett, Ruby Dee, Katherine Dunham, Roberta Flack, Aretha Franklin, Nikki Giovanni, Dorothy Height, Lena Horne, Coretta Scott King, Gladys Knight, Patti LaBelle, Toni Morrison, Rosa Parks, Leontyne Price, Della Reese, Diana Ross, Naomi Sims, Tina Turner, Cicely Tyson, Alice Walker, Dionne Warwick and Nancy Wilson.

The historic weekend began Friday with a private luncheon at Oprah's Montecito home where the "legends" were greeted by the "young'uns" including Alicia Keys, Ashanti, Angela Bassett, Halle Berry, Mary J. Blige, Brandy, Naomi Campbell, Mariah Carey, Natalie Cole, Kimberly Elise, Missy Elliott, Tyra Banks, Iman, Janet Jackson, Phylicia Rashad, Debbie Allen and Alfre Woodard, among others. Throughout the weekend, the "young'uns" paid homage to the "legends" for their great contributions. World-renowned event planner Colin Cowie attended to every detail, and Grammy Award-winner John Legend performed his hit song, "Ordinary People."

On Saturday night, it was an elegant white-tie Legends Ball with notable guests including Sidney Poitier, Tom Cruise, Katie Holmes, Usher, Barbra Streisand, James Brolin, Lionel Richie, John Travolta, Kelly Preston, Diane Sawyer, Mike Nichols, Maria Shriver, Chris Tucker, Barbara Walters, Quincy Jones, Spike Lee, Senator Barack Obama and Tyler Perry, among many others.

The finale of the Legends weekend was Sunday's exuberant gospel brunch with spontaneous performances by Patti LaBelle, Gladys Knight, Dionne Warwick and Chaka Khan.

Being on standby to grab sound from any one of the amazing women at any time was exciting, to say the least. I first began to get words from the guests in front of Oprah's home at the group portraiture sitting helmed by Kwaku Alston, photographer to the stars.

You've heard the expression, "I can die now." Well, that's how I felt after that splendid weekend at Oprah's estate. White folks had Truman Capote's Black and White Ball and now black people were getting the Legends Ball.

These were the women who'd told my story, my mother's story and my sister's story on screen. They'd helped me celebrate the best moments in my life and their voices had provided me comfort while being heroic in their own personal lives.

Think of Legend Tina Turner. For years, she was a victim of domestic violence and professional exploitation from her then husband, Ike, until one day she'd had enough. In the divorce settlement, she gave Ike her share of everything except for her iconic stage name. Such a decision came from Nutbush City Limits, Tennessee-born Anna Mae Bulloch, whose talent and drive transformed her life of childhood abuse and poverty into one of rock & roll and domestic abuse. Still, she would continue to stretch and grow and show up to finally find her bliss. I related to her story of going way beyond the past to find oneself.

In 1978, my family had moved from our last install as an Air Force family in the Norton Air Force Base in San Bernadino, California to Savannah, Georgia. This was where my parents' childhood home had been and it's where they wanted to retire. Savannah in the late '70s had a modest tourist appeal, but indicators of its rebirth began to show up with the founding of the Savannah College of Art & Design, which began to refurbish the city's historic buildings for classrooms and labs. For this little black boy who'd already seen the world as an Air Force brat, the move to Savannah seemed premature and stifling. Progressiveness wasn't always felt or expressed by my brown people and I'd begun to hear the murmurs, "Black folks in Savannah, stay in Savannah." There was this sentiment in many of the nooks I frequented in my new hometown that aspiring beyond a job that paid just above minimum wage with benefits, was not the thing to do. From many I saw before me, their dreams consisted of staying put or going up the road to the big city of Atlanta. Even for those who tried to get away, I saw them come back and they were often depleted from the hand that life dealt them. I wondered, "Was my childhood travel in the Air Force going to be the extent of my seeing the world?"

Diving into the pages of reference books showed me a world that I could continue to dream of while my prepubescent feet were planted on the ground for the next ten years in Savannah. Reading about my favorites, like Tina Turner, helped me know that she not only got out of St. Louis to travel all over the world as Ike's lead-singing half, but later transitioned to a whole new level of stardom via her determination and spiritual practice of Buddhism. Artistically, she took chances that took her to the top of the global charts throughout the '80s with hits like, "What's Love Got to Do With It," "Private Dancer," "We Don't Need Another Hero, Thunderdome" and "The Best." She accomplished all this in her late 40s, even after many had counted her out from ever returning to the industry in a reputable way.

After a breakthrough transforms you, you can be who you want to be and go where you want to go. Tina Turner ultimately chose Switzerland as her place of residence with her beau of twenty-seven years, Erwin Bach, whom she married in July 2013.

I'm thirteen years into a loving partnership with a fabulous man named Anthony. As many try to define when we should get married, as if it was legal when we first got together, we look to Tina and the choices she has made for her life as inspiration that you can do matrimony as you want to do it. No apologies and not by committee, but by our rules.

Think of Legend Maya Angelou, whose expression of a "caged bird" gave this little black gay boy from the Bible Belt hope that one day he might sing out loud. At the age of eight, Angelou was sexually abused and raped by her mother's boyfriend, a man named Freeman. She told her brother, who told the rest of their family. Freeman was found guilty but jailed for only one day. Four days after his release, he was murdered which was probably done by Angelou's uncles. Angelou became mute for almost five years after that. She believed, as she stated in her first autobiography, *I Know Why the Caged Bird Sings*, "I thought, my voice killed him; I killed that man because I told his name. And then I thought I would never speak again because my voice would kill anyone."

As a young child of eight or nine, I experienced a slew of inner turmoil from my awareness that I was gay. I was raised in a household that was very religious and with so many fingers pointing to this line or that line from the Bible exclaiming that if you're gay, you're going to hell. Wanting to please my parents and not bring them any stress, I kept my truth at bay. It would be another fifteen years before I could become comfortable enough to come out to friends. And another five years passed before I felt safe enough to come out to my family. But just like little Maya, I knew this caged bird would find the words. And I did!

Again, think of Legend Shirley Caesar and her interpretation of the song, "No Charge," which would lyrically prepare me for my mother's passing when I was twenty-three years old. Though she was gone too soon, her sacrifice for me was "paid in full."

Think of Legend Roberta Flack. Among the albums I would check out from the Savannah's public library when my dad would take me, was Roberta Flack's *First Take* which included the transcendentally tender ballad, "First Time Ever I Saw Your Face."

I've experienced a sense of rapture about so many of the Legends including iconic model, Naomi Sims and the equally-legendary Young'uns like fellow fashion goddesses Iman and Naomi Campbell.

When Aretha said "Respect" and Lena told Dorothy to "Believe in Yourself," I got right in step as a child. The Queen and the Good Witch had spoken.

My mother disciplined just fine, but a good read from Phylicia Rashad as Claire Huxtable would get me right in line as well. In syndicated repeats, they still work.

Rashad's sister, Debbie Allen, who told you how to achieve fame is the same Debbie Allen who stood on the shoulders of choreographer, Katherine Dunham, who'd passed away before the Legends special aired the following year.

And here they were. Many were moved by the experience and sharing their feelings as such. Cicely Tyson spoke to me from her lunch seat as she held court. Some of the other Legends were kneeling to greet the acting icon as if she'd pulled Miss Jane Pittman from the grave to sit with us and catch up. At the end of the luncheon, where most of the Legends and Young'uns were exiting the gazebo under which the meal took place, Tina Turner said she didn't think she'd ever see these women again, so she was grateful for the moment.

They were all so beautiful. It was a wonder that the absolutely gorgeous Mariah Carey wanted to make sure she had extra light and the forever youthful Janet Jackson, who wore faded and torn jeans to the lady's luncheon, wanted to get in the shade. Halle Berry figured all light was good on her. The sparkle from the freshly-placed black and white hoop earrings that Oprah gave all of the Young'uns may have been providing Halle some of her external glow.

After these three amazing women and many of their fellow Young'uns gathered to recite Pearl Cleage's commissioned poem, "We Speak Your Name," Miss Ross told me in my ear that, "Angela Bassett could read the phone book and I'd cry." At the gala, seeing Miss Ross and Smokey Robinson dance to Michael McDonald and Ashford and Simpson on, "Ain't No Mountain High Enough," was next level. Still, all eyes were on then Senator Obama who, with Michelle Obama, was a welcome guest for the historic night. Tom Cruise and his new girlfriend, Katy Holmes, enjoyed the evening calmly this time as it had been a week since he'd jumped on Oprah's Chicago-based couch, proclaiming his love for Holmes.

Bebe Winans wrote, produced and debuted a song called "Legends" that he created with each and every honoree in mind, referencing "Reach Out and Touch Somebody's Hand" with Diana, for example. Near the end of the song, Oprah called out the names of all the Legends in attendance and as the audience was already standing, the Legends stood one-by-one. There wasn't a dry eye in the house.

The glory continued into the next day. For those who had never been to church, they got the pure essence of it on Oprah's lawn that Sunday morning where my boss introduced the worship phase of the celebration. Wintley Phipps performed a moving "Amazing Grace" while the Legends and Young'uns broke bread together and just enjoyed the afternoon. Bebe Winans created a magical moment in which he, along with Edwin, Tramaine and Lanette Hawkins began to sing Tramaine's "Change." BeBe floated through the audience on the lawn, handing the mic to some of the Legends and Young'uns who didn't come to play but were ready. Natalie Cole jumped on the stage and joined the Hawkins as back-up. Shirley Caesar, who initially wasn't going to be able to make the gospel brunch, secured a replacement at her home church and started the spiritual jam off with her freestyle vocal arrangements. From there, the mic just floated from diva to diva including Patti LaBelle, Gladys Knight, Chaka Khan, Yolanda Adams, Valerie Simpson and Dionne Warwick. Mariah Carey even hummed a little ditty, though she cautioned that the hour was too early for her seven-octave range. In all, we had a gospel explosion on Oprah's front lawn. On a lighter note, Kennedy royalty, Maria Shriver joked with me that she was happy they didn't hand the mic to her during the revival.

In one moment of sadness, Ms. Warwick and I spoke of the missing diva in the room, her little cousin Whitney Houston who was invited to honor the Legends but couldn't make it. I didn't know any of the details then, but history shows that 2005 was a difficult year for the diva whose struggles with drugs began to intensify during this time. Several in attendance including fellow songstress Patti Labelle, spoke her name with the tones of care and concern you'd expect from a loved one. Many of the women brought her up as an obvious absence and sent prayers her way. The world's next impression of Whitney would be on her husband Bobby Brown's reality TV program, *Being Bobby Brown*, which ran on Bravo. Houston was a prominent figure throughout the show, demonstrating to most that things weren't good.

My only regret from the weekend, and it is an enormous one, is that I didn't take a single picture. Not even one of me in my hotel meticulously going over my notes on the guests. For as long as I've been in the industry, thirty years now, I am never without my camera. I never forego the opportunity to capture the moments that I grew up seeing in magazines, but this weekend wasn't about me. It was about these women and the opportunity to consume what I'd waited my whole life for.

So much of my life, and what has gotten me through, is woven into these wonder women. First and foremost, I am a journalist. My job is to tell the truth and get an accurate story but in truth, my heart is in telling the uplifting story. Let someone else cover the sordid details regarding the woman's prosecution, jail time and the fall from grace. I'm not interested in that as I don't want to tell you about Martha Stewart's incarnation as Snoop Dogg's partner-in-crime. I want to admire the glorious talent of Vanessa Williams who continues to deliver on all platforms. I want to tell you about the first sound of the phone ringing on her debut single of "The Right Stuff," her Grammy-worthy ballad of "Save the Best for Last," her tour de force Broadway show, *Kiss of the Spider Woman*. Not to mention her more recent TV work in *Ugly Betty* and *Daytime Divas*. I want to confess how I still weep at the sound of Whitney Houston's voice, a legacy of vocal excellence that will live forever.

My confession is that I'm a journalist but also a fan and this is a love story.

chapter 2

Visionaries

One of the greatest honors of my life was when Berry Gordy requested me to host *Motown the Musical's* opening night in New York City. "He has a memory of steel, B.G.," Miss Ross said about me to Mr. Gordy as they came forth on the red carpet, after walking down 46th Street upon exiting their limo. Indeed, it was a superstar moment seeing Mr. Gordy and his muse together again!

The musical is set in 1983 at the Pasadena Civic Auditorium, focusing on the final dress rehearsal for the show to celebrate the 25th anniversary of Motown Records. The narrative centers on Berry Gordy who everyone is looking for, but no one can find because he's back at his hotel reminiscing about his creation. Though the musical focused on Berry Gordy, everyone remembers that Michael Jackson owned the anniversary show and that Diana Ross was the First Lady of Motown, returning for the first time since leaving the only label she knew domestically for a lucrative $20 million contract with RCA.

My family and I watched *Motown 25: Yesterday, Today, Forever,* during May sweeps before we caught up with the times and bought a VCR, so I audio taped it. I can hear our family's cheers and screams for the Jackson 5 reunion and then Michael Jackson's moonwalk. I'd already heard that there wasn't going to be much of a Supremes reunion, but I was excited to see it just the same. You can hear my family's peanut gallery commentary on each greeting as Miss Ross called various Motown legends onto the stage. "Oh, Michael sure loves him some Diana Ross." My mom said. "See how they kissed and embraced?" She added.

Apparently, Michael was fond of Berry Gordy. After Miss Ross called him down from the balcony to the stage, Berry was met at the edge of the stage by the most famous Jackson who hugged him for at least thirty seconds. "Okay, Michael. That's enough Michael!" my dad screeched as we watched all of the Motown stars sing along to the final Diana Ross & The Supremes No. 1 song, "Someday We'll Be Together." When I'd play *Motown 25* via tape, I always wondered why that long hug between Michael and Berry bothered my dad so much so that it warranted a break-the-fourth-wall shout at the TV. I remember it made me uncomfortable as this was also a recording that connected to my sexuality and what constituted as an acceptable masculinity. Such declarations were actually on tape and not just in my head.

But watching this amazing finale unfold on stage, I had more on my mind than Michael Jackson's hug of gratitude to Berry Gordy. I imagined Valerie Simpson whispering into the diva of the night's ear as she had through Miss Ross's headphones during recordings of her solo albums in the '70s. Much of which Ashford & Simpson produced including her first No. 1 hit, "Ain't No Mountain High Enough" and the monster disco single and album title track, "The Boss."

Valerie Simpson along with her husband Nick, was responsible for many of Motown's biggest hits as well. Marvin Gaye was particularly fond of working with them. He and Tammi Terrell scored many hits together in the late '60s starting with the Ashford & Simpson gem, "Ain't No Mountain High Enough" in 1967. Ashford & Simpson continued to produce chart successes for this favorite R&B pairing. After Tammi Terrell was diagnosed with a malignant brain tumor that led to her death in 1970, Valerie provided vocals to Motown's release of the beloved duet's third album.

I admire Valerie a great deal, and I've asked her about how she creates a song. I'd imagined that the process always happens with her behind the piano in her studio with a pen and paper in hand, but she's said just the opposite, that "brain spark" actually happens anywhere and everywhere. "I just try and stay aware," she said.

There was another wiz behind the curtain at Motown who was largely responsible for the enormous production consisting of a thirty-six-member cast, twenty more folks in the pit and sixty arrangements. The latter being a mere fraction of what was cranked out of the Motown hits factory.

Berry was at the top of this, but Suzanne de Passe was at the center. After being introduced to Berry by her friend Cindy Birdsong who was Florence Ballard's replacement in the Supremes, Suzanne rose from a lowly assistant at Motown to being Berry's partner and a close friend of The Boss. She proved it's not where you start but where you end up and eventually she would go on to serve as Miss Ross' wedding matron of honor. After Motown was sold, Suzanne formed Gordy/de Passe Productions with Berry and was the subject of two Harvard Business School case studies. Thus, proving the Motown hits factory was, above all else, a business and a woman was running it. She won a 1983 Emmy for *Motown 25*. She earned yet another Emmy for *Motown Returns to the Apollo* in 1985 which was the same year she bought the rights to Larry McMurtry's Western Novel, *Lonesome Dove*. She was determined to turn it into a CBS mini-series. In 1989, the program aired, and *Lonesome Dove* became the most popular mini-series in five years on the network. It brought Motown more than $10 million in profits and earned de Passe yet another Emmy nomination. De Passe Entertainment would eventually house her next productions from the late '80s through the '90s including 1987's Showtime at the Apollo with twins Tia and Tamera Mowry's hit show *Sister, Sister* and their spin-off starring their brother Taj in *Smart Guy*.

Suzanne isn't a rare breed in this respect. Black women have been entrepreneurs, creators and innovators since the antebellum era to now. Visionaries I've marveled at include Susan Taylor who during her tenure as editorial director of *Essence Magazine*, envisioned what has become Essence Festival and the biggest music and empowerment event targeted at African Americans. Initially the 1995 Essence Festival was designed to be a one-time salute to *Essence Magazine* on its 25th anniversary of serving an audience primarily comprised of African-American women.

What has always inspired me about Susan Taylor is her knack for incorporating her spirituality and disciplined manner into everything she does. I've spent time with her in her office and her penthouse apartment as well as taking a walk together in Central Park. Regardless of setting, she was centered, never stuttering through a single question. I remember after our 6 a.m. walk in the park, she wanted to change from her athletic chic attire into her "*Essence* woman" business look. Our second shoot would chronicle her at the *Essence* office when they were in the heart of Times Square. She'd answered all my questions and I had more for her once we got to her office. I just couldn't resist letting her know that my personal favorite quote from her helped me exorcise toxic friends from my life in my 20s.

"Everyone is not healthy enough to have a front row seat in our lives." Goes the quote. "There are some people in your life that need to be loved from a distance." She thanked me graciously and she was curious to know if the diagnosis worked. I assured her it had, though making such a move hurt a few people's feelings. "But how much have you done with your life?" she asked. "Tons more than I would have with those negative reinforcements around." I replied. The guru she was to me, at this time in my mind, was pleased as she excused herself to change for our second location.

I got the opportunity to be a personal escort for Oprah Winfrey as a part of Susan Taylor's fundraiser for her mentoring organization, National Cares, in December 2008. Her team asked me to volunteer. I was assigned to work closely with Ms. Taylor's VIP guests including Ruby Dee, Congressman Charles B. Rangel, Sean Combs, Michael Eric Dyson, Sheryl Lee Ralph, Roland Martin, Rev. Al Sharpton and Phyllis Yvonne Stickney. Yolanda Adams, Donnie McClurkin and I would be on private detail with her special invited guest Oprah who donated $1 million that night to the cause. The evening started at a private reception at Ms. Taylor's home, just off the Westside Highway in one of the high rises that once carried the Trump name. The well-appointed affair was well thought out for a main event at ESPACE. "We can do better." Susan Taylor said to the room of enthusiastic guests. Her energy inspires her employees as well as any others who come into contact with her.

Another person I admire is my dear friend Robbie Montgomery who began her career in the 1960s as an Ikette. The Ikettes were the backup group for soul duo sensations, Ike & Tina Turner. In fact, she danced and sang behind Tina, doubling as a sister friend. "When I left St. Louis with Ike and Tina, I had all these dreams of being this big-time singer." Miss Robbie told me in 2014. "I'm still waiting." She said. But she had her day in the spotlight, leaving Ike & Tina behind after the domestic violence between them got to be too much. Moreover, the newfound spirituality Robbie found through Buddhism would have her introduce the practice to Tina before she left.

"Everybody was saying Tina doesn't want to remember her past." Robbie offered. "I was her past and when I left Ike & Tina, I had to leave her, and she was like a sister. It was touching to see Tina tell Oprah that she considers me a special person." This was shared with Oprah in an August 2013, sit-down interview that Oprah conducted with the diva while in attendance at her wedding to beau-of-twenty-seven-years, German producer Erwin Bach. According to Tina, Robbie gave her shoes and money while they were on the road, during which time Ike was said to be severely mistreating Tina. After Robbie's lung collapsed, she could no longer sing so she returned home to St. Louis, gathered up her mother's soul food recipes and created Sweetie Pie's. On the strength of her business acumen and solid recipes, Sweetie Pie's is an iconic St. Louis soul-food restaurant with multiple locations. Its docu-series on OWN-TV, *Welcome to Sweetie Pie's*, was considered a game-changer for the fledgling network in 2011. In it we saw the relationship between Robbie and her son/business partner, Tim, who'd been locked up for ten years. And though they fuss and fight, they demonstrate the palpable ways in which family can work together via excellence and second chances.

For all of their highs, Miss Robbie has also suffered through some horrendous lows including the St. Louis murder of her grandson Andre. But what she continues to demonstrate is a strength and a resilience that must come from the chitlin' performing circuit. Miss Robbie is tough, but she is also sweet.

Her story makes me think of other visionaries, unflinching in their path. Lisa Price wanted to do one thing, but her customers wanted something else. She loved creating fragranced soaps and skin products and began selling them at flea markets, but black women kept asking if she had any products for their hair. Before long, she was giving them what they wanted in the form of Carol's Daughter which is a company that sells natural hair and beauty products for African-American women. Price got a big boost when Oprah mentioned the company on *The Oprah Show* in 2002. Web traffic soared and soon celebrity investors like Jay-Z, Will Smith and Jada Pinkett Smith had jumped on board. Annual sales of Carol's Daughter eventually skyrocketed to $30 million. L'Oréal USA stepped in and offered Lisa a deal she couldn't refuse. The acquisition was met with bullying on Twitter from disappointed fans who loved that the business was black-owned. As an entrepreneur and a creative, what stands out to me is this germ of an idea, took shape from her kitchen and over time and favor, she leveraged her business to attract investors and a buyout that any smart businessperson would welcome. This, while keeping the integrity of her products as well as the expanding line made Lisa Price an inspiration indeed.

A double dose of entrepreneurship, innovation and creativity also comes from Miss Jessie's, another company that sells natural hair products for curly, coily and kinky hair. The grandmother of Miko and Titi Branch inspired their enterprise. With a Japanese-American mom and African-American father, Miko and Titi had problems finding salons to care for their textured hair. They started doing it themselves while perfecting their paternal grandmother's homemade hair products. In 2004, the women were just getting over their failed beauty salon in downtown Brooklyn when they came up with the idea for Miss Jessie's. Working out of their Brooklyn brownstone in a basement salon and creating a products laboratory in the kitchen, the women were able to cultivate great success.

 I met Miko Branch at the well-appointed ballroom called Cipriani, located on 42nd Street, for a winter holiday gala in 2014 benefitting the Doe Fund. Our mutual friend Andre Robert Lee served on the board of directors which provides work and job training to hundreds of formerly homeless and incarcerated individuals. They highlighted how much more the program has thrived as being more than just a shelter. We all donated to the cause via several opportunities to give inside the evening. Andre sat Miko Branch next to me as he felt we'd hit it off and we did. Before we wrapped it up, we exchanged information and Miko agreed to sponsor my upcoming karaoke open-mic with free Miss Jessie's goody bags and full-sized product as well.

 "Titi is going to love you." Miko said to me about her sister as we got to know each other that night in late November, 2014. Miko hipped me to what could be expected from their business memoir for Harper Collins and Amistad, *Miss Jessie's: Creating a Successful Business from Scratch, Naturally*. The tale would chronicle how they achieved their multimillion dollar success in the natural hair care industry of curls, kinks and coils. She told me that they do speak of their sacrifices at the beginning of starting a business as they co-parented Miko's son, Faison. She also pointed out that, at times, she and her big sister Titi didn't always get along. However, they learned through their own mistakes and lessons how to resolve their differences and keep the business thriving. Their product line, the code of which was cracked in their kitchen sink when Titi came up with the right blend for their first product "Curly Pudding," became one of the bestsellers for Miss Jessie's.

 That was November 30, 2014. By the next day, Miko made sure our Miss Jessie's bags were sent for our weekly karaoke event's run.

She'd invited me to the Miss Jessie's holiday party which was coming up the second week of December. However, literally a few days later, word hit the streets that Miko's sister Titi Branch was dead, reportedly by suicide. A rush of sadness hit me and remains even until this day because I'd only just met Miko a few days before Titi died. I was still supposed to meet her and hit it off.

Before I knew it, we were postponing when Miko would visit our karaoke night. Instead, she asked if I'd sing Patti LaBelle and Sylvester's "You Are My Friend" for Titi's memorial the following month in Brooklyn. She was asking me to be the sole singer for Titi's funeral. It felt so personal and I had to deliver.

A month later, on the morning of the memorial, I walked into a packed church of grieving people. Among them were women who called Titi a friend because she was devoted and loyal. There were a host of clients and customers from over the years who'd considered Miko and Titi's chat rooms and YouTube tutorials for maintaining natural hair to be just what the doctor ordered.

When it came time for me to sing, I said a quick prayer first. Spirit led me to say a few words. "I never met Titi and I wondered what Miko meant in asking me to sing this challenging song in particular." I said to the audience. "But as I look around and see all of your faces and as I hear all of the stories, I see that Titi was a friend to so many of you and so is Miko. And indeed, they were each other's best friend." All went well with my delivery of the song. What I didn't expect is everyone to jump to their feet and sing along with me, for Titi, as the song calls for a choral refrain.

Having experienced a degree of that tragedy, amidst their company's reigning success, underscored for me that Miko would grieve as she and her family found out more about the reported depression that Titi had been managing in silence for many years. Moreover, Miko continues to show me she is strong and knows how to push through her challenges. She has heart and, channeling the legacy of Titi, she wants to continue to be generous with it. I rarely question her decisions because she tends to know a moment when she sees it.

If she can stretch and get it together then so can I and so can all of us.

And there are more stories, some tragic and others uplifting. To paraphrase Beverly Bond, Black Women Rock! The world-renowned DJ and former model founded Black Girls Rock in 2006. In 2010, Bond partnered with BET to televise her groundbreaking awards show which showcases and celebrates the breadth and depth of women in the African Diaspora. The program, a perennial No.1 ratings draw among black households and an NAACP Image Award winner, has attracted former first lady Michelle Obama as a presenter and Congresswoman with Maxine Waters as an honoree. I love Beverly Bond's love of girls and women and the action she continues to take to lead in their uplift.

All of these black girls rock.

SCRAPBOOK

The former **Essence** editor-in-chief, Susan Taylor, founded National CARES Mentoring Movement, a community-based movement offering tangible support to African Americans in low-income and unstable communities.

I often run into Susan Taylor socially in New York City, typically at movie premieres and galas. Here we are in March 2012 at the United Negro College Fund gala held at the Times Square Marriott Marquis where R&B diva Ledisi performed a lovely arrangement of "What a Wonderful World."

When I first moved to New York City in the mid-90s, the restaurant owned by former model B. Smith was the place to dine in the theater district when seeing a Broadway show. Here we are catching up December 2007 at the World Premiere of The Great Debaters in New York City at the Ziegfeld Theater. A few years later she announced she was suffering from early onset Alzheimer's.

In April 2015, storied magazine editor and author, Harriette Cole, asked me to be a guest on her web series **The Root: Bring it to the Table**. Our discussion of the pleasures and pitfalls of fame was seamless as Harriette and I have known each other for years – from her days of editing the pages of **Essence** and **Ebony**.

Being named one of the most spiritually influential people in recent years is a far cry from being born Rhonda Eva Harris in the early '50s in Brooklyn, New York. After a difficult childhood and adolescence, Rhonda was renamed Iyanla, which means "great mother." After her Yoruba tradition anointing, she went on to thrive – eventually becoming a lawyer. But her calling was and continues to be the uplift of others.

Although Iyanla Vanzant and I worked for **The Oprah Winfrey Show** in the late '90s, I only met her in August 2015 in Minneapolis where she was promoting her Oprah Winfrey Network show, **Iyanla: Fix My Life**.

I produced the history video for The Links Incorporated's 65th Anniversary. The organizers were so pleased with my work, they invited my partner Ant and me to enjoy the gala and view my work on the big screen in Washington, D.C. We were pleased to meet member, Linda Johnson Rice, of the former publishing empire responsible for **Jet** and **Ebony** magazines.

I met Yvette Noel-Schure in the late '90s as she was a Sony publicist representing Jessica Simpson, the fashion designer who was then a full-time recording artist. Eventually she would rep Destiny's Child and continues to work for its lead singer Beyoncé. Here we are at an after party celebrating opening night of the Broadway musical Chicago starring Destiny's Child member Michelle Williams.

One night after dining at Yuki 55, Black Girls Rock founder Beverly Bond and her husband Bazaar popped upstairs where I was hosting a Karaoke fete. It was the first of many encounters. Here we are at Brooklyn Community Services Gala in June 2013 supporting writer and women's advocate Michaela Angela Davis at the Grand Hyatt in New York City.

Ant and I with Beverly and Bazaar in January 2012 at the **Red Tails** Premiere in New York City.

chapter 3
Miss Ross and Other Gay Icons

In 1970, the year of my birth, Diana Ernestine Earle Ross, left the Supremes behind and began a solo career. The group had numerous hits during the '60s, becoming Motown's most successful act, the United States' most successful vocal group and one of the world's bestselling girl groups of all time. The Supremes released a record-setting twelve No. 1 hit singles on the U.S. *Billboard* Hot 100 including "Baby Love," "Stop! In the Name of Love" and "Someday We'll Be Together." Diana Ross had risen from the projects of Detroit and became one of the world's biggest entertainers proving that hard work, dedication and readiness are essential tools for success and longevity. But Miss Ross still wasn't satisfied and none of us should ever should be.

After the release of her eponymous debut solo album which contained the top 20 pop hits included "Reach Out and Touch Somebody's Hand" and the No. 1 pop hit, "Ain't No Mountain High Enough," she became a movie star. Her first feature film was 1972's, *Lady Sings the Blues* which was based on the life of jazz singer Billie Holiday. When I saw the movie some years later and realized she'd lost that year's Best Actress Oscar to *Cabaret*'s Liza Minnelli, I walked around sulking for days. The *Blues* soundtrack of course reached No. 1 on the *Billboard* Hot 200 Albums Chart.

Then in 1975, Miss Ross starred opposite Billy Dee Williams in the love story, *Mahogany*, with Williams having appeared in the Holiday biopic as well. Again, the accompanying soundtrack produced a No. 1 hit, the introspective ballad, "Do You Know Where You're Going To?"

I truly came into awareness of Miss Ross with the release of her 1979 and 1980 albums, *The Boss* and *diana*, with the latter featuring the international hit, "I'm Coming Out." I was ten at the time and unsure what it meant to be gay or to come out, but the track would become an anthem in later years. Black music legends Bernard Edwards and Nile Rodgers of the disco group, Chic, wrote the song and intentionally included Morse code to "the family." Though not gay themselves, the song was inspired by their time hanging out in New York's hip, trendsetting gay clubs. Here they noticed quite a number of Diana Ross drag queens. So, the song was written with the idea of Miss Ross singing it as homage to her gay fans. And we are legend!

"The only people who like Diana Ross are white or gay." Said a straight male friend of my sister, Janice, as I was planning a watch party for the HBO filming of Miss Ross' Motown comeback tour in 1989 from London's Wembley Arena. I wasn't out to anyone, or to myself yet at this time, so I wondered to whom this young man was referring. As a fan, I'd seen Miss Ross perform countless times, from Atlanta to New York City to Atlantic City to Denver and beyond. The first time I connected with her, I was front and center at the Fox Theatre in Atlanta. She approached the edge of stage while singing her top 20 hit, "Dirty Looks" from *Red Hot Rhythm & Blues*. This was her final album for RCA and the label that plucked Diana from Motown for an unprecedented $20 million recording contract. With authority, she pointed to me and said, "You know every lyric!" I got a rush and was transfixed.

In 1997, after seeing another dozen or so shows between Atlanta and New York, I had another Ross run-in at Madison Square Garden where the Grammys were held. I managed to get a ticket and happened upon Miss Ross as she was entering the Natural Museum of History for one of the after-parties. Her daughter Tracee was nearby and waved to me. During this time in New York City, you could always run into Miss Ross' girls, Rhonda and Tracee, at a fun VIBE event or industry set.

"I love your pants." Miss Ross then exclaimed while pointing to my black, white and burgundy houndstooth pants which were made by the Brooklyn-based Nigerian designer Moshood. I might have gotten a "Thanks" out but kept moving through the crowd to my table. It was too tight a scene to engage her any further as there were onlookers, servers and photographers roaming about.

In 2002, I'd have another run-in with Miss Ross which clarified for me that she knew I was one of her true fans. I was a guest of *Upscale Magazine* for its new cover party at Flute Lounge in the Ironbound area of New York City. The cover subject was Tracee Ellis Ross, who attended with her dad Bob Ellis and mom, all of whom held court in a private nook of the club. As security was escorting Miss Ross out of the venue, we caught each other's eyes.

"Miss Ross!!?" I said sheepishly. "Yes! I know you..." she replied. At the same time, her team was pulling her away from me. "Stop!" she said to them. "I want to talk to him!"

Now what was I going to say? I went on to let her know that I'd be seeing her June show at Westbury Music Fair in the round which was one of my favorite ways to experience a Diana Ross show. The stage is in the center and surrounded by seats on all sides. She joked that she wasn't sure if she was going to be doing that show, though I assured her I had the tickets. "Here I am booked for a show and I don't know if it's happening or not." She said, and we laughed. She hugged me goodbye and I was moved. Weeks later, she did do that show. I remember someone yelled out for her to do, "Love Child." She said they weren't prepared to do the song, but she'd look at the sheet music. She glimpsed it, cued the band and did a perfect version of my favorite Supremes No. 1. She never disappoints!

A couple of years later, I heard that Diana was going to be giving a benefit concert for the Arch Street Teen Center in Connecticut's

Roger Sherman Baldwin Park. This was where her sons Ross and Evan spent their afterschool time. Therefore, she wanted to do something nice for the center. I was beginning to come into my own as a tastemaker and pop culture guy around town, so I simply requested a media ticket to attend and handle further coverage of the fundraising campaign and of course, the show. The Arch Center called with my access and I was eventually seated front and center. Miss Ross played a nineteen-song set list, a third of which were Supremes' hits. I was sporting red and white hand-painted drawstring pants with a pink tank top, and she was led to call me on the stage to dance with her on her scintillating No. 1 dance hit from 1980, "Upside Down." Did she know it was me? I wasn't sure but we danced like we were 1970s' Michael and Diana, getting down on her debut TV special. Then Miss Ross almost made me faint as she escorted me off the stage.

"You always have the best pants!" She gushed. I could have died and gone to heaven, but I'm glad I didn't because she then sang, "The Boss" which was one of my favorite Ashford & Simpson-composed tunes from the album of the same name.

By the time I actually got to interview her at Oprah's Legends weekend, I felt like we were old friends and her willingness and excitement to talk to me was proof. When I asked what was on her heart, she said she was so moved at the intergenerational part of the experience. She said there was representation for each decade that weekend from the '20s to the '90s. In mentioning the singer Ashanti, as one of the babies on deck, she accidentally called Aaliyah's name. She quickly corrected herself and it touched both our hearts. That Freudian slip informed me that Aaliyah surely would have been invited to tribute the Legends if she hadn't died in August, 2001 in a plane crash after she shot a video in the Bahamas.

"I can't let you walk away from me without you telling me who you're wearing." I said to the always fashionable style icon who then swirled around for me. She was showcasing a beaded strapless gown with mid-chest cutouts wrapped in something satin and tulle and all black.

"You know I'm a designer." She said, because she knows I know. "I get dressed at the last moment and put a lot of different outfits together. So, I don't just put one designer on."

Every time I'm in Miss Ross' realm, whether as part of an audience or face-to-face, is a total honor. Certainly, there's something mystical to her presence. She was the inspiration that made the hard days manageable. All I had to do was put on her, "Be A Lion" from *The Wiz* and I'd be recharged for the next hurdle from childhood to adulthood. She continues to be a moral compass for me, and I've continually leaned on the historic Central Park Concert as a metaphor for my life. When a torrential thunderstorm poured down twenty minutes into her free show, she sang triumphantly in the rain until she made the realization that she would come back the next day. "I've made the decision. We'll do it tomorrow!" she exclaimed.

When the next day came, the weather was beautiful, the park was full, and Miss Ross declared to the audience both in New York and worldwide that, "It's a new day!" That affirmation has sustained me and gotten me out of the bed on many days.

Contrary to popular belief, interacting with Miss Ross in the flesh has been a dream every time. Knowing that I'm towing a thin line between fan and entertainment journalist, I once said to Miss Ross during the Legends weekend at the Bacara Resort & Spa where all of the honorees resided for the legendary weekend, "I can't keep running into you like this, Miss Ross! My heart just drops!"

She laughed as she sat in a golf cart that was preparing to drive her to her destination.

Diana and her light had been there for me when I was a child. I think deep down, I always knew I was different from others. I didn't know to call that feeling being gay, but it did show up sometimes as a never-spoken attraction to a boy or a magnetism for glitz, glamour and divas. Though, this is by no means a given when it comes to being gay. Miss Diana Ross was my muse then, and decades after, she continues to be a candle in the dark for me. Over the years, whenever I'd match her high notes, flip an invisible tress of hair that wasn't there or spout off the Supremes' latest accomplishments, it became clear that my adoration of Miss Ross was more than a passing crush on a childhood idol. I would come to understand many years later that she is my gay icon. Not too unlike the Beyhive and Lambs of today who chase after Beyoncé and Mariah, I obsessed over Diana Ross. Whatever she did, I had to see it, buy it, hear it and have it at my disposal at all times. When I needed to cry, she had, "Didn't You Know You'd Have to Cry Sometimes?" A rare Ashford & Simpson gem that they cut for her third solo album *Surrender*. "Missing You," the posthumous Marvin Gaye homage that Lionel Richie wrote for her on her 1984 album *Swept Away* was also a go-to for me.

For variety, Miss Ross gave me pop, ballads, country, jazz, standards and as we moved through the '70s and into the '80s, disco/dance and modern R&B. Additionally, the European and Asian markets began to pluck major hits for her after America put in its expiration date on veteran artists having hits, par the course on these shores. In her life's narrative, Miss Ross didn't always think she was the boss. There was insecurity on her part when it came to her voice, her looks and her worth. For her to find her calling and, with seemingly razor-sharp focus, turn that into such a stellar career has continued to impress me until this day.

Diana and all my other divas have offered a safe place of sorts. An escape into their feminine realm which isn't perfect but seems to welcome the weigh-in of the LGBTQ community. Miss Ross has always loved her gay fans.

I've always cherished Miss Ross but as mentioned before, I didn't always self-identify as a gay fan. In the '70s and '80s, I had managed my internal feelings to mirror the "norm." I had no shortage of well-intentioned loved ones willing to correct me from walking and talking "like that." Flouncing was unacceptable as was singing in falsetto and twirling my imaginary hair. I dodged as best I could the taunts like "sissy," "punk" and the dreaded f-bomb. In church I stuck with using my lovely baritone while reserving my powerful falsetto for the shower. In my desire to not rock the boat as a teen, I was blessed to have feelings for a wonderful young lady named Rachel, who would later be extremely supportive of me when I came out many years after we broke up. We are the dearest of friends today and forever bonded.

As socialization goes, I had to go to the prom and debutante balls. This kept relatives comforted and bullies at bay. Even after graduating from Morehouse, I was still in the closet. I became a reporter trainee at the ABC affiliate in Atlanta for WSB on Channel 2, which further informed my need to butch it up as one college adviser had stated that my "way" wouldn't translate well on the news desk.

But by my mid-20s, I knew my experiment in alternative truths and pronouns was no way to live. And through undeniable pain, I eventually found the courage to come out. As Diana would sing in "It's My Turn,"

> "I can't cover up my feelings in the name of love, or play it safe, for a while that was easy. And if living for myself is what I'm guilty of, go on and sentence m., I'll still be free..."

So, the gradual embrace of larger than life figures were huge. Miss Ross wasn't the first and isn't the only icon to embrace gay culture. She's spoken openly of gay clubs she's attended and how the boys would sometimes carry her around above their heads. Fast forward to 1996, when she honored her LGBTQ following by producing "A Night of 1,000 Dianas," hosted by drag queen extraordinaire RuPaul for Miss Ross' Motown remake of Gloria Gaynor's, "I Will Survive." I also remember reading an interview with Miss Ross in which she said if any of her kids were gay, she would continue to love them. I always imagined that as my mother's sentiment since she would pass away before I could officially come out.

Gay icons connect with us through entertainment and advocacy, but they must also be fierce, glamorous, and talented. We want them to give us an anthem to sing at the top of our voices and present unforgettable style. It's Toni Braxton and Jennifer Lopez in low-cut and thigh-high Versace. Dolce & Gabbana did Whitney's 1999 tour wardrobe which was major! And hair is a big part of the equation.

There's a lot of it, says Diana Ross and Chaka Khan, or sport it short, says Grace Jones or Rihanna.

Most importantly, they must be advocates for us.

Dionne Warwick was an early and vocal ally to LGBT people. During the '80s, when most were scared to say AIDS, Warwick got President Reagan to say the word as the disease went rampant and could no longer be ignored by the government. Dionne says she was losing so many industry friends including makeup artists, hair people and designers. She knew she had to position herself front and center in the movement. She repeatedly donated her singing and fundraising talents to high-profile charity events. In 1985 she rallied music-royalty such as Elton John, Gladys Knight and Stevie Wonder to record, "That's What Friends Are For." This was in order to raise money for amfAR, an AIDS research organization. The song hit *Billboard*'s No. 1 spot and raised more than $3 million.

Dionne came into my consciousness as host of the '80s television music show, "Solid Gold" which I watched religiously. I now adore her work that precedes my birth, namely the Burt Bacharach and Hal David compositions that include "Walk on By" and "I Say a Little Prayer." Her '70s outing with the Spinners, "Then Came You," gets me dancing every time I hear the tune. And her Barry Manilow-penned work, "I'll Never Love This Way Again," in many ways kicked off her tenure at Arista which brought her back into popular favor. Over the years, I've had the chance to meet Dionne and experience her as a lovely lady who truly cares about people. She also commands respect and has no problem letting you know.

Other gay icons maintain their place in my circle. In my household, I live with my partner Anthony. Just as there's little you can say to me when it comes to Diana, ditto for Anthony and Janet Jackson. She has been quite a friend to us. Her 1997 album, *The Velvet Rope*, which is among Ant's favorites, featured lyrics that openly explored homosexuality and bisexuality among other taboo topics like bondage, depression, isolation in the internet age and domestic abuse. The song, "Together Again," which references friends she lost to AIDS, was a big hit. Moreover, on the album Janet speaks and sings openly about desiring women on one interlude while her Rod Stewart, "Tonight's the Night," remake and the funky "Free Zone" take on homophobia and LGBTQ love.

Whenever Ant and I are in her company which is usually at a promotion for a record release or movie premiere, Ant can hardly contain himself. After Oprah teasingly threw a damp rag to Ant that Janet had used to blot her sweat during a performance of her *20 Y.O.* single, "So Excited," Ant was over the moon with excitement. He's framed the rag!

Another diva who doesn't mind snapping for the kids is Beyoncé. She had us even before she embraced her Sasha Fierce persona, but she sealed it when she played Diana in *Dreamgirls*. Well, she actually portrayed Deena Jones, a character loosely based on Diana Ross and the Supremes. Imagine my pleasure after we completed our pre-show meet and greet with Beyoncé in Manila where Ant took me for my birthday in 2007. After we had someone snap a shot of our Filipino hosts and us with Beyoncé, she acknowledged my birthday.

"You have a good one!" she said, referring to Anthony being my man. "Yours is good too," I said back, referencing Jay-Z with whom she wasn't yet uber-public about. Ant added to our quick chat and said, "Don't forget to snap for the kids."

"I won't forget to snap for the kids." She said. "Where are you guys sitting?" Ant shared our location and before I knew it, her amazing show flew by and she was coming towards our section, exclaiming, "Where are my boys from America?" She looked out. "This is for you." From there, Beyoncé sang me "Happy Birthday" while Ant and I held each other and cried.

This moment lives in our minds and firmly in my heart. Beyoncé has been there for the LGBTQ community throughout her career. In September 2017, she gave transgender actress Laverne Cox a gig modeling in the fall campaign for her athleisure line, Ivy Park. Her music video, "Formation" also incorporated Big Freedia, Messy Mya and gay slang into the creative mix. Beyoncé has acknowledged that her hairstylists and makeup artists inform the language she sometimes incorporates into her music, like "slay," a popular gay term which often honors African-American women who present with authority and high style. Beyoncé's choreographer, Frank Gatson, introduced the diva to a style of dancing known as J-Setting which originated from the female dance team of Jackson State University, an HBCU located in Mississippi. Eventually much of the gay culture of the South adopted the style of dancing created by the Prancing J-Settes of Jackson State as showcased in the short-lived Oxygen reality series, *The Prancing Elites Project*, in 2015.

Wearing unitards reminiscent of the scene, Beyoncé executed the J-Setting dance moves of strutting and tiptoeing in a uniform fashion during her Sasha Fierce period, as seen in the *Billboard* Hot 100 chart-topper, "Single Ladies" as well as "Diva." Moreover, she has embraced Frank Ocean as a duet partner. When Frank Ocean revealed his bisexuality to the public in 2012, Beyoncé was one of the many artists showing her support. Ant and I later sat next to him in the front row of Beyoncé's sold-out *Lemonade* show in Rutherford, NJ.

Like Beyoncé, so many of our female entertainers appreciate the LGBTQ community. One year, the guests at Black Pride in New York City were lucky to get Miss Deborah Cox and Patti Labelle for their big South Street Seaport circuit show. Patti delivered to the fans the look that she made so popular as "a do" in the '80s, when her stylist Norma Harris pulled her hair back, pressed hair pieces flat and arranged them around her head to look like a flying saucer or the crown of the Statue of Liberty. The style was wild and over the top, and first introduced on her "New Attitude" video which was connected to the *Beverly Hills Cop* soundtrack.

In addition to taking the fans back with her look, she sang all her songs including "Lady Marmalade" and the obligatory kicking-off-her-shoes highlight, "Over the Rainbow." Patti's LGBTQ allegiance precedes any drag queen that imitates her in the club shows all over the nation. Both Patti and fellow LaBelle bandmate, Nona Hendryx, say they knew they were on the right path in their early days of singing their first hits, "I Sold My Heart To The Junkman," "Danny Boy" and "Down The Aisle," as enthusiastic drag queens gave them validation.

Nona Hendryx is bisexual and was always the most outspoken of the trio which also consisted of Sarah Dash. As a songwriter, Nona helped to set them apart from other girl groups. As they renamed themselves simply Labelle and threw out the dresses and bouffant wigs for jeans and afros, Nona's contributions to their next albums, 1971's *Labelle* and 1972's *Moon Shadow*, brought material that included sexual and political subject matter. This was unheard of at the time for an all-female black group.

Though Patti missed the group's early-era ballads, she acquiesced. Nona became the chief songwriter for most of the act's records. She wrote powerful ballads such as, "You Turn Me On," "Nightbird" and "Going Down Makes Me Shiver" as well as a wealth of more uptempo numbers like "Space Children," "Messin' With My Mind," "Gypsy Moths" and "Who's Watching the Watcher." In 1974, the group hit gold with the release of *Nightbirds* following the release of the smash hit "Lady Marmalade" with futuristic outfits in tow. Not many black women, let alone openly bisexual and Buddhist black women like Nona, were making their presence known. However, Nona always did it out loud and unapologetically.

In 2008, Nona performed with True Colors, a musical tour created by popstar Cyndi Lauper as a way to empower the gay, lesbian, bisexual and transgender (GLBT) community to reengage and take part in the struggle for full equality. Nona had her finger on the pulse during her Labelle days and made sure Patti and Sarah supported the movement.

Whatever the reason, these women feel like friends. I'm grateful to each of them for giving me an escape from the loneliness that can sometimes come from knowing you're gay but having no outlet to communicate your experiences and desires. These icons keep bringing us inspiration through their recordings, live shows, television appearances, and films, also speaking to their own drive and ambition. More times than not, they're making sure they perform for their loyal

LGBTQ following who will support them through all of their good and bad days and album releases. And I appreciate their attention and the acceptance.

SCRAPBOOK

Ant and I with Beyoncé and company at her 2007 concert in Manila, the capital of the Philippines.

I've interviewed Mariah several times, notably during Oprah's Legends weekend and again while she was promoting her **Touch My Body** project. She also introduced me to her then manager, Benny Medina. I took this picture of her and her, then husband, Nick Cannon in August 2013 at the Premiere of Lee Daniels' **The Butler**. I was there helping Colman Domingo manage red carpet interviews along with co-stars Oprah Winfrey, Cicely Tyson and Jane Fonda.

Jody Watley has been my muse since her days as a Soul Train dancer, and then with the group, Shalamar. My fondness grew when she embarked on a solo career including dance floor bangers, "Lookin' For A New Love," "Real Love" and one of the first hip hop ditties with featured rappers Erik B and Rakim, "Friends."

I danced the night away with Jody at a 1995 journalist convention show in Philadelphia dubbed "Night of Dazzling Divas." Jody often invites me to her shows in recent years, one of which landed on Diana Ross' birthday. Jody obliged me with a cover of Miss Ross' "Love Hangover" and said from the stage, "I hope you're satisfied. I remixed my set for you!"

Jody Watley backstage at BB Kings Supper Club where she gave a sold-out show in February 2015 and March 2016.

The esteemed Dionne Warwick has excelled as a singer, actress and TV show host. With songwriting partners Burt Bacharach and Hal David, Warwick is second only to Aretha Franklin as the most-charted female vocalist of all time. Fifty-six of Warwick's singles made the Billboard Hot 100 between 1962 and 1998. Of course, "That's What Friends Are For" is my favorite!

I spoke with the legendary Ms. Warwick at a press conference and preview of **Ain't Nothing Like the Real Thing**, an exhibit about New York's iconic Apollo Theater in February 2014. She signed a copy of her autobiography, "My Life as I See It." Knowing I was covering the media event, I made sure to have my book handy as celebrity biographies and autobiographies are among my favorite literary genres.

I first met Aretha Franklin in the summer of 1993 while on assignment for my first job at Good Day Atlanta. We chatted about her favorite, The Young & The Restless character, Victor Newman at the Ritz Carlton during her Chastain Park Concert after party. Crowned the most charted female artist in the chart's history, the Queen of Soul stays rooted. She once had hired me to find some full-figured girls who were mimicking Beyoncé's "Single Ladies" to perform at a Christmas party in Detroit and paid me with money she took from her bosom!

In Fall 2012, I was among an intimate group who joined the Queen of Soul for the preview of Motown the Musical on Broadway in New York City.

Aretha Franklin's birthday party in New York City. March 26, 2016

In her career of 50 years, Patti LaBelle has been inducted into the Grammy Hall of Fame, Hollywood Walk of Fame, Apollo Theater Hall of Fame and the Songwriters' Hall of Fame. As an actress, starred in movies, television sitcoms and lifestyle shows. I've encountered her as a fan and as a journalist. As an avid fan, I went to see a number of her shows back in the 1990s and early 2000s. Fast forward to 2008, I was one of those sitting in the **Divas with Heart** concert featuring her, Chaka Khan and Diana Ross. As a journalist, I did an interview with her, and boy was it a memorable one! I remember I was already in Philadelphia back then, just minutes away from her home. Then my crew gave me a heads up that she may not be in the mood because a good friend of hers had just died. Turns out it was Gerald Levert who had a heart attack. They had performed together many times in the past. At one point during our chat, she got one of her new gospel CDs, signed it for me, and even played it!

Patti LaBelle and her LaBelle bandmates met up summer of 2008 at Splash in New York City to promote their anticipated reunion album.

My favorite diva, Diana Ross, grew up in public housing in Detroit. She went on to become a star of the stage, the screen and the voice of Motown. In 1973, she received a Golden Globe and an Oscar nomination for her portrayal of Billie Holliday in the biopic **Lady Sings the Blues**. She had won many American Music Awards before receiving the 2017 Lifetime Achievement Award. And she earned twelve Grammy nominations before being honored with the Grammy Lifetime Achievement Award in 2012. In addition to receiving two of the highest U-S honors: Kennedy Center and the Presidential Medal of Freedom, she has two stars on the Hollywood Walk of Fame.

I remembered that Miss Ross' Hollywood Star on the Walk of Fame was right in front of the Egyptian theater where I'd invited a handful of L.A. friends to meet me for a screening of one of my favorite Ross films , ,"Mahogany." In this summer of 2009 when I was post-producing episodes of "Monica: Still Standing" and "Frankie & Neffe" for Dubose Productions, I was excited to see one of my guilty pleasures on the big screen. But in good conscience, before I could enjoy my movie, I bought a toothbrush and some cleanser to shine her up.

MISS ROSS AND OTHER GAY ICONS | 53

As Miss Ross was wrapping up a sold-out tour of one-nighters across the U.S., I was thrilled to be invited on stage with her in New York City at The Waldorf. We didn't pose, but just stared into each other's eyes admiringly.

I was delighted to host **Motown: The Musical's** opening night celebration and interview all the guests as they walked the red carpet. Here I am catching Berry Gordy and Miss Ross. They were joined at the performance by original Supreme, Mary Wilson, as well as Smokey Robinson, Stevie Wonder, Gladys Knight and many of the other Motown Legends.

I first fell in love with little Janet Jackson as she performed alongside her siblings on a CBS summer variety show with their name on it. Soon, the sitcom camera began to love on her from playing Penny on Good Times and Charlene on Different Strokes. In her teens, she started recording music including her debut project, Janet Jackson and the follow-up Dream Street. Her 2017 State of the World Tour was a major success and a comeback in the wake of her having a baby boy at 51 years old.

Janet Jackson in 2009 at the Bryant Park Hotel's Cellar for the New York premiere of Tyler Perry's, "Why Did I Get Married?"

Opening night reception at NYC's Lehmann Maupin Gallery in October 2010. The exhibition featured moving still-images of the cast of For Colored Girls, Tyler Perry's latest drama. Janet Jackson hosted the event.

chapter 4

Angels

It is always difficult for me to hear when women leave the world at a young age because their passing reminds me of my mother. She died of a heart attack at the young age of fifty-three. Mom was the first diva I loved. She was a church singer as I already mentioned, and my dad was one as well. He was big on the gospel quartet sound like the legendary Dixie Hummingbirds. And my older brother Herman and I seem to have gotten those gifts handed down through DNA. Because my dad had us traveling all over the globe via the Air Force, mom's home church in Savannah couldn't always be the backdrop for her singing. Somehow, though, wherever we were, folks would find out that mom sang, and they would book her down-home gospel for whatever affair they could.

Thomas Dorsey's pioneering hit "Precious Lord" was one of her staples. One time, in San Bernardino, the local school was preparing an opening ceremony for its brand-new library. It was a big deal for the community. The organizers knew of my mom's talents and instead of asking her to do her usual genre of gospel, the request was for her to do a pop ballad called "You Light Up My Life." Debby Boone did a beautiful job with that *Billboard* No. 1, a classic that underscores brilliantly the lite FM sounds of the time. Mom wanted to do the song justice but didn't want to run from a riff here or there to make it her own. As she rehearsed, I weighed in on which of her chosen nuances were working. My mom and I gave feedback to each other as singers. That was our way.

Mom's singing wasn't the only way she distinguished herself from her Savannah peers. She'd also lived overseas during my dad's time in the Air Force. Honestly, even her stint in San Bernadino was impressive to the local women for whom a drive to Atlanta was a rare adventure. She'd also been a star among the military wives and always had ideas for a special program, community event or fundraiser. She didn't smoke or drink but was still considered a cool chick with a snatched together hairdo or wig. Mom carried a rubenesque stature that she playfully and halfheartedly tried to shed. During her stint in Tokyo, she and her girlfriends on the base would attend a TOPS (Taking Off Pounds Sensibly) meeting then they would enjoy a meal at their favorite eatery in the local market afterwards. TOPS was originally formed in 1948 as a response to the need for assisting overweight and obese people to lose weight by setting up a support group system. I was always in the cut, cheering mom on to hit her marks and to maintain her healthiest weight. She won some. She lost some. Prior to her dying, she'd let her previous health scare two years earlier jolt her into getting it together. And she did, though her heart would still eventually give out.

Maybe I'm being dramatic because I'm the baby of the family and feel that twenty-three years old is too young for a "mama's boy" to lose his mom. After all, I hadn't yet begun to live and fulfill the dreams she had for me. The ones only she seemed to understand. She knew I had my eye on the prize and encouraged me to hit the mark accordingly. So, everything that I pursued before she died had the heat of her encouragement. When I was asked to do an introduction at the CBS Special *Kennedy Center Honors* with the Morehouse College Glee Club, Mom ensured that the local press knew about this young Savannah resident doing great things.

A couple of weeks before my Morehouse graduation, my mom fell ill with congestive heart failure. The news came the very day I was scheduled to rehearse for the next day's Miss Morehouse pageant which I was hosting. Once my sister, who lived in Atlanta, called about my mom's condition, we rushed to be by her side in the ICU. I fell to pieces when I first saw her with all of the wiring and prods. But calmly and deliberately, she said to me, "Don't cry. They're taking care of me fine. But don't you have an event to host tomorrow? And what about those final things you have to take care of for graduation?" Since I had my eyes on her and there was nothing more I could do, Mom insisted I leave my sister there and hop back in the car to get back to Atlanta for my business. Her parting declaration moves me to this day: "And I'll be there at your graduation in two weeks."

It wasn't an easy road, but mom and her Jesus took the wheel and got her to Atlanta to see her baby boy become a Morehouse Man.

Since I immediately had a job as a reporter trainee at WSB-TV, Mom made sure my transition into the workforce went smoothly. She helped me find a place and underwrite what the entry level position couldn't accommodate. Mom was in much better shape since it had been over a month since her congestive heart failure scare. In addition to getting me out, I could sense her working on herself to make sure she'd be there for the next rungs of milestone. But I still wondered if Mom knew more than she was telling us.

By the end of that year, I'd won an Atlanta Association of Black Journalists' Award for a freelance feature I did on Aretha Franklin at the top of the summer. The Queen of Soul was doing her first Atlanta concert in eleven years and had returned to the dance charts with club banger "A Deeper Love" and to the top 40 with the Babyface-penned "Willing to Forgive." The well-appointed event took place at former President Jimmy Carter's iconic Carter Center which has been a human rights force. Mom loved that too as she was Team Jimmy Carter.

Dressed to the nines for the award ceremony, Mom was sparkling in a sequined top with a matching headband. She elegantly coupled it with a simple black skirt and her high heels which hurt her feet all the time. Although, you wouldn't know it while she was out and about. Knowing I approved of the glam she brought to the occasion, Mom was proud to see me receiving an industry honor for covering one of my favorite divas, though not Diana. She also got to meet my new coworkers at competing station WAGA-TV where I had been hired as an associate producer for *Good Day Atlanta* which launched my career of interviewing celebrities. Aretha was one of my first. As our station at the time was a CBS affiliate that carried mom's and my favorite soap, I made sure to ask Ms. Franklin her thoughts on the latest plot on *The Young & the Restless*. She responded enthusiastically, even imitating the show's villain, Victor Newman, as she dished. Mom high fived me as that excerpt from the piece showed on the big screen at the ceremony. The audience roared in laughter and applauded. Through that sea of validation ushered by my mother, I walked up to the podium to receive my award.

Mom was always excited when I was doing what I said I wanted to do since childhood. Her support and enthusiasm were felt and just what I needed as it wasn't easy to be as young as I was and reaching for the stars. But mom was always the safe space I could land before she'd push me back out there to go get my prize. My vision was to hit the mark where I could buy her an expensive car or thank her with an Emmy in hand or something that everybody could see.

Even though she'd been ill for years, I was shocked by her death as I was always expecting her encore. Fast forward to July 20, 1994. I was producing on Atlanta's hit morning show *Good Day Atlanta*, which had several nominations in the mix that year for the National Association of Black Journalists Salute to Excellence Awards, as well as the Southeastern Regional Emmys. I got a few of my interviews on the air including clips with En Vogue, Aretha Franklin, Babyface and TLC. Mom was always so proud and that made me want to do more and to keep going.

I was beginning to try other things to set my next steps in motion. I was one of the co-chairs for the first Unity Journalists of Color conference scheduled to take place at the end of July in Atlanta which was hosted by the Atlanta Association of Black Journalists. For this, I was a vice president. In addition, I'd go on to be one of the youngest to sit on the NABJ's board. I also began to expand my brand, singing in media friends' weddings and also for special events. I even took on some small acting roles where I could fit them in, landing a background part in Spike Lee's *Drop Squad* and a couple of music videos for LA Face Records. This included an unreleased version of TLC's "Creep." Even if mama had to blink to see me, she was always so into my trajectory. I also had joined in with several of my childhood friends to start a summer camp called Options: Image of the Future with the mission of providing scholastic support to kids.

At the end of the second summer, we were soon to wrap up camp for 1994. I did get some family time in a couple of weeks prior for Independence Day weekend. My mom came up from Savannah with family, so we could go to a picnic thrown by my sister Janice's law firm where she worked as a legal secretary. We all went out to Lake Lanier and had the best time ever. My mom went back to Savannah after the holiday.

After a day of Good Day Atlanta, the summer camp and a car repair errand, I made it home around 3:30 p.m. absolutely exhausted. Then my brother called. "Hey! Boo, Fe, and I just got back from the movies and found mom breathing funny." He said, referencing his son Herman and his son's mother Felecia. "The ambulance just came and took her to the hospital. Y'all need to come on!"

I froze, the ensuing emotions familiar because of what happened two years before. But this time, it didn't feel like we were going to be as lucky. I called my sister who was still working downtown and shared the news. She said she'd come and get me. The plan was that we'd rush to her place in Lithonia, let her get her bag together and go. Once we got to her home she was accompanied by her fiancé Vincent, so I chose to stay in the car while they popped in to put a bag together. I sat in the backseat of my sister's Nissan in a fetal position, hoping the feeling of devastation would pass.

Then my sister's dear friend Jackie came out to the car. "Patrick?" she asked. I locked the doors. I wasn't sure why but if I was going to receive bad news, I was going to hold it off for as long as possible. Then Vincent came back to the car with the keys, opened it up and told me I needed to come in and check on my sister. As I reluctantly walked up the stairs to her apartment, I hit my fist into her building's wall. No one told me Mom had died but I just knew. I walked into the house and my sister was devastated. I was in shock and in no place to comfort her. I was a zombie, I was checked out.

The next hour or so was a blur. It would take that time for us to gather ourselves and hit the road for the three-and-a-half-hour drive from Atlanta to Savannah. I eventually went back to my fetal position on the ride home to Savannah and by the time we arrived, I awoke to Lionel Richie's voice singing "Father, help your children and don't let them fall by the side of the road." I'd never listen to the Commodores' "Jesus is Love" the same way again.

To be honest, I've been broken ever since Mom's death. But she prepared us for this early on, reminding us that she wasn't supposed to live past eight years old as she was a sickly child with Rheumatic fever. But prayers and faith would have her remain here for almost another fifty years to be the amazing force she was in the world.

"I lost my best friend," I offered the packed church of loved ones from near and far who came to celebrate her life. I took a stab at singing one of her favorites, "Wind Beneath My Wings." As the well-intentioned pianist tried to keep up with my impromptu performance, I gestured for him to stop "plunking" behind me so my final song to mom could breathe. The incident was dramatic but after some reflection, my family placed it in our funny file of memories of things we observed on that horrifically sad day. Certainly, Mom was laughing from on high. I had to sing my song right for my girl.

Immediately after we buried mom, I came back to Atlanta to move forward with business as usual for the Unity convention preps. I pushed through that deadline and a few more that were on the calendar in August 1994 before I emotionally crashed and wound up needing to talk to a grief therapist. I hoped to enroll the rest of my family in as well, so we could heal together after such an integral loss. No one took my recommendation. Instead, we all found our way to healing independently. Though we were still a close family, with mom removed from the axis, our bond would never be the same.

A few months after mom's passing, I made the decision to leave Atlanta for New York City due to a job offer. By Valentine's Day 1995, Dad helped me pack my car and drove me to my new life. As our brother would be in and out of trouble with the law, my sister and I developed an adult closeness with each other. The bond has been compromised by the parts of us that continue to hurt and haven't healed. The pain is the same, hitting us in different places and at different times. In turn, we are not always each other's safe place. I attribute this dynamic to us not participating in grief counseling together.

As the only female Riley left, my sister tried to take on maternal roles like cooking for Thanksgiving and Christmas. Each experiment was met with thumbs downs from the fellows because we were hurting so much that we couldn't celebrate what my sister was trying to do. We were just longing to have mom back. It was hard to be there, emotionally, for each other during this sad time.

Though my nephew was five years old when his granny passed away, one day a year or so after mom's passing, the family and I were doing some shopping in Walmart when all of a sudden, he started crying. "I miss Queen Riley." he screamed out loud. We all did. We all do.

Several years ago, at the premiere of *Life's Essentials with Ruby Dee*, I remember feeling so envious of Ruby Dee's grandson, Muta' Ali Muhammad, who'd spent years interviewing her. And now, just after her passing, he was left with a trove of video footage, family photos and memorabilia of his grandmother. I had only a few pictures and what was in my heart and mind.

Why can't every black woman have the life of Ruby Dee who was vibrant even at 90? Sure, we shed sentimental tears when she died but mostly we rejoiced because we knew she was joining her soulmate of nearly 60 years, Ossie Davis. Talk about a full career and a full life. She was an actress, poet, playwright, screenwriter, journalist and Civil

Rights activist. In 1961, she originated the role of Ruth Younger in the stage and film versions of *A Raisin in the Sun*. Among her awards were a Grammy and Emmy and she was eventually presented with a National Medal of Arts and Screen Actors Guild Life Achievement Award. I was delighted whenever I got to interview or entertain with her because, in spite of her storied career and political focus, she was still fun. We even shared a box of popcorn at the premiere of Halle Berry's film *Frankie & Alice*.

I have been blessed to personally know some of the most talented women the world has ever produced. These women were larger than life to their fans, but they were just as vulnerable to life's tragedies. Too many of them died too soon. The unexpected loss of someone famous with millions of fans is always mournful but when they are young, and the death could've been avoided, it's particularly heartbreaking.

I wasn't even thought of when the jazz singer Billie Holiday died penniless except for the $750 magazine payment for her life story taped to her leg. She was only forty-four when she succumbed to liver and heart disease in 1959 while under arrest in her New York hospital room for illegal possession of narcotics. But the music left behind and the gut-wrenching portrayal of her by Diana Ross in *Lady Sings the Blues* make me feel as if I personally experienced Billie's death the way I have with other songbirds.

I was actually huddled over my phone with a group of friends watching a (streaming) presentation of Diana Ross receiving her Grammy Lifetime Achievement Award when "Whitney Houston is dead..." popped up on my handheld.

The human condition is so strange. In that moment, I tried with all my being not to register what had appeared on the screen. I'd been so happy to see Diana Ross finally get her due having never received a Grammy award, either with the Supremes or solo, in spite of her twelve nominations. But I couldn't keep my grief at bay. I became inconsolable. Years of drug abuse had taken Whitney down.

If there was a person to whom the original pop female superstar had passed the torch, it was Whitney. Diana's career and persona seem an obvious blueprint for Whitney; the long formal concert dresses, the ladylike appearance and the eventual move to film. Where Diana was brought along by Berry Gordy, Whitney had music pedigree. Her mother, the singer Cissy Houston, cousin Dionne Warwick and family friend Aretha Franklin for whom Cissy sang backup as part of the Sweet Inspirations. While Whitney couldn't rival Diana's longevity, discipline or decorum, her career was unparalleled. Two hundred million records sold worldwide and the only artist to chart seven consecutive No. 1 Billboard Hot 100 songs. In her film debut, she co-starred with Kevin Costner in the romantic thriller *The Bodyguard* in 1992 and sang the soundtrack hit "I Will Always Love You." A Dolly Parton tune which received the Grammy for Record of the Year and Album of the Year, becoming the bestselling single by a woman in music history.

I remember being introduced to Whitney by the recording artist, Pebbles, who was a friend from my days in Atlanta. We were in New York City at the London Hotel, adjacent to the Ziegfeld Theatre, when I walked into the lobby to see Whitney, stunning in a two-piece white tux and turtleneck. She'd just announced she was pregnant with another child after Bobbi Kristina and we were all going to walk next door for the world premiere of *A Preacher's Wife*. This was nearly a decade before we witnessed the musical goddess devolve into a drug-fueled abyss on a TV reality show with her husband, Bobby.

Whitney died only a few miles from where Diana was receiving her award, a few floors up in the Beverly Hills hotel from where she was expected to appear that night at the pre-Grammy party of her mentor, music executive Clive Davis. She was preparing for a comeback. Instead, Whitney Houston was dead at 48.

R&B songstress Vesta Williams sang on par with the greatness of Whitney Houston but from the "Unsung" section of the diva list, Vesta struggled with image and weight issues while slimmer and more mainstream icons like Whitney, Janet Jackson, and Vanessa Williams were at the top of the charts during this time. Great vocal talent, notwithstanding, it was the music video era.

Though never a Billboard chart-topper, Vesta was a singer's singer. She was known for the legendary rendition she did of "The Star-Spangled Banner" at a Los Angeles Lakers game for which she used four octaves of her vocal range. The singer had lost one hundred pounds in the months before her death in 2011 of an enlarged heart. I've always admired the vocal prowess she exhibited in her work including her signature "Congratulations" and her top five R&B hit "Special." As well as "Once Bitten, Twice Shy," an up-tempo top 10 number she released that continues to be my jam today. Vesta comes from the vocal school of Chaka Khan who hired her along the way. I loved that she did commercial work including the McDonald's advertisement with Al Jarreau where she bebop's like Ella Fitzgerald. And her hums and belts on the theme song to the *Women of Brewster Place* miniseries makes it worth seeing every time BET shows the program.

Another vocalist who suffered through hard times was Natalie Cole. Even though she was one of the few performers of her generation to have been born with a silver spoon. By twenty-five, the daughter of the legendary crossover music sensation, Nat King Cole, she was an R&B star in her own right. She'd later act and sing jazz and standards on her way to selling thirty million records before her death of congestive heart failure at sixty-five, after recovering from decades of drug addiction that included heroin and crack cocaine.

As favorites go, she has always been on the list. When our family was stationed at Norton Air Force Base in San Bernadino, California, Janice and I got to see Natalie in the first concert I ever attended. And she's been a childhood favorite since then. I think because my sister was transitioning into her teens, I mimicked her enthusiasm for Natalie in our sibling talent shows. My sister was a girl, she loved music and the sassy black women singers were her favorite. So, Natalie Cole's debut single "An Everlasting Love, This Will Be" and "I

Got Love on My Mind" got nonstop play on our record player in the '70s. At this time, Natalie Cole was giving Aretha Franklin a run for her money as all of her material was written by Chuck Jackson and Marvin Yancy whom she'd eventually marry. Suddenly Natalie was moving in on the territory of the Queen of Soul. Even one time, going so far as to say she could sing rings around Diana Ross.

Well, I certainly wouldn't go that far, but Natalie could wail. By the time the gospel-tinged anthem "Our Love" came out in 1977 on Natalie's *Thankful* album, I must have been coming into my own. I no longer automatically gave the vocals to my big sister. I was beginning to enjoy gospel music, choir songs in particular. The track's frequency helped get me in touch with my falsetto and how it hits right in the key of Natalie. To this day, "Our Love" is known in my karaoke circles as "Patrick's song."

But even after Natalie fell from grace in the late '70s and success evaded her, she inspired us all by returning to the pop charts with an '80s sheen. "Jump Start" was an up-tempo synth number that spoke to the youth. We saw a clean and sober Natalie in the video looking revived and dancing in a studio, juxtaposed with images of skaters and vendors on Venice Beach. From there, she'd have my attention and I'd continue to appreciate her rung of hits including the ballads, "I Live for Your Love," "Miss You Like Crazy" and her remake of Bruce Springsteen's "Pink Cadillac."

And yet another comeback occurred for Natalie when she chose to sing the duet "Unforgettable" with a recording of her father as a lead-off single to an album featuring remakes of his material. That full circle moment for her would bring much joy to two generations of fans and garner for Natalie more Grammys and notoriety than she'd ever had in her long career.

On December 30, 2015, we were about to close out our last All-Star Karaoke for the year at Harlem hot spot, Billie's Black. We were preparing to take a break until we picked up our weekly Tuesday night in spring 2016. The faithful folks who come out to my Harlem open mic wanted one more song. They chose "Our Love" and I sang it. Two days later on January 1, 2016, I awoke to the news that Natalie Cole had passed away. Gone too soon.

Natalie Cole's autobiography is titled *Angel on my Shoulder*. Now she and the other ladies are among them.

SCRAPBOOK

While in Los Angeles to attend the African American Black Film Critics Association's Oscar Viewing Party in February 2013, I stopped by the Grammy Museum to see the Whitney Houston exhibit.

Ruby Dee was a celebrated actress and civil rights activist whose career traversed various platforms in theater, radio, television and film. Despite slim odds due to her race, she succeeded in fulfilling her dream of becoming an actress. Apart from numerous awards, she is credited for being the first African-American woman to play lead roles at the American Shakespeare Festival. She is also known for being a leading cast member in soap operas in the 1950s and 1960s, a rare feat for an actress of color. Even at the age of 83, she was nominated for an Oscar for best supporting actress due to her role in the 2007 film **American Gangster**. She left an unquestionable legacy. In her final moments when she passed at the age of 91, she was in the company of her family and friends.

Ruby Dee and I at the special screening of her upcoming film **Frankie & Alice,** November 2010, at Cinema 2 in New York City.

Here we are again in 2010 at Alvin & Friends, a Southern/Caribbean contemporary bistro in New Rochelle, New York. A photographer approached us for a picture but as she was getting up, I actually asked her to stay seated so I could kneel.

Natalie Cole passed away on December 31, 2015 at the age of sixty-five. Coincidentally, two days prior to her passing, I'd wrapped up my Billie's Black presents All Star Karaoke season with Ms. Cole's classic "Our Love," a tune I've been singing since childhood and every week at our spirited open mic night! It always inspires as will the life and legacy of Natalie Cole. I continue to pay tribute to her canon and on any given Tuesday, I might perform "I Live for Your Love," "This Will Be," "I Got Love on My Mind" and "Jump Start" or "Unforgettable."

Here I am seated at Miss Cole's request between her and my good girlfriend Sidra's twin sister, Tasha Smith, at Harlem Fashion Row's 5th Anniversary at the Jazz at Lincoln Center during Mercedes-Benz Fashion Week, September 7, 2012.

In 1986, I was drawn to Vesta's voice which to me was reminiscent of Chaka Khan's. When I first saw her in video form on club bangers "Once Bitten, Twice Shy" and "Don't Blow a Good Thing," I thought she even looked like Chaka Khan. As I would find out, she sang background for Chaka in the late '70s and early '80s. I wasn't surprised when I saw this big-and-bright-haired beauty in the video for her smash hit ballad "Congratulations," a quiet storm anthem in the voice of a woman whose former lover is marrying another woman.

In the early '90s her record sales slowed down, and she lost her recording contract. She decided to lose one hundred pounds and take on acting work. Though Vesta would continue to work for years including spots in commercials and movie themes and appearing as a spokesperson to bring awareness to childhood obesity, she never peaked. She was found dead in a Los Angeles hotel room.

In 1995 in Philadelphia on the stage of a showcase called "Night of Dazzling Divas," Vesta invited me to dance with her for one of her early hits "Don't You Blow A Good Thing."

The untimely death of Sidmel Estes Sumpter was a great loss to me. Sidmel was not only the first woman to preside as president of our beloved National Association of Black Journalists but also the first person to take a chance on me. As executive producer of **Good Day Atlanta**, she hired me as a reporter trainee from WSB-TV. This was my first step to becoming a pop culture expert and entertainment reporter. When I left for New York she explained that she LOVED having me at **Good Day Atlanta** and considered me one of her NABJ "babies." This was a term of endearment. The death of one of my industry moms saddened me.

Sidmel and I always had to take a picture at the annual NABJ Convention. This was taken in New Orleans in 2012.

My mom, Queen Elizabeth Bellinger Riley, is a Savannah native and a preacher's kid. She spent all of her childhood and teenage years in the church, though she did have an interest in performing and theater in high school. A year after she graduated high school, my dad asked for her hand in marriage. In 1980, my dad retired from his 27-year career in the United States Air Force. Along the way, they set a distinction of having three kids born in three different countries. My sister Janice was born in Savannah in 1963 before Dad sent for her and my mom to join him in Berlin, Germany, where my brother Herman Jr. was born two years later. In 1970, I was born in Tokyo, Japan. Wherever we were stationed, our mom was super popular and very much a mentor to many including other Air Force wives.

I love to say my mother was my best friend from the womb. As the baby and the most sensitive one of her three offspring, I always felt like mom treated me extra special. Turns out, after talking to my siblings, they felt extra special too. Having each of us feel unique and special was Queen Elizabeth Bellinger Riley's gift to us.

In 1970, I was born in Tokyo, Japan where my Air Force father was stationed. As my mom tries to feed me on the couch in our living room, I'm drawn to the click of dad's camera. Even until this day, I have to get the shot, and the work done, before I can eat at ease.

Though a church singer from Savannah, Georgia, my mother's talents were known globally. Since my dad, she followed him to Germany, Japan, and all over America from 1961 to 1978. This performance was February 1976 at the Norton Air Force Base chapel where mom was the featured vocalist for a Black History program. She sang one of her staples, "Precious Lord Take My Hand."

My dad served in the United States Air Force for 27 years. Here's a family shot we took on Moody Air Force Base in Valdosta, Ga in the mid-'70s.

This is the last picture I have with my mother. She drove up to Atlanta where I lived for a Fourth of July cookout in 1994. Other family members and friends got in on the fun that day. She'd return to Savannah the next day and die a few weeks later on July 20, 1994.

chapter 5

Women on Broadway

Broadway is seen by some as out of reach. Though Manhattan is a twelve-mile island, the little neighborhood called the theater district between 40th Street and 52nd Street, framing the actual street named Broadway, has been hiring African Americans since the early 19th century to present. In the early 19th century, minstrel shows were the genre of the day. This is where that tradition of white actors in black face, and often times black folks in white face, comes from. Thus, highlighting racial stereotypes and creating broad-stroke judgments on our supposed behaviors, demonstrations of us being silly, never serious and what some might call "coonish." The producers on these shows were white and held control over creative players and salaries. They often hired black artists to execute a particularly reductive vision of our character.

By the 1930s, the Great White Way was ahead of its time in employing African-American workers and performers. *Porgy and Bess* is arguably the best-known black musical ever. Though it had only a short run in 1935 due to criticism of its lightweight score, operatic recitative and most importantly to the African-American community, its focus on negative black stereotypes involving drugs, gambling and loose sex, it now has an esteemed place in history thanks to a revival staring Audra McDonald. She was the winner of six Tony Awards and the first person to win all four acting categories.

Broadway has highlighted the African Diaspora and African-American culture through landmark plays and musicals like *A Raisin in the Sun, Fences, Dreamgirls, Ain't Misbehavin', The Wiz, Bring in 'da Noise and Bring in 'da Funk*. It has truly shined a spotlight on black actors. Consider that about forty black women have won a Tony compared to only eight who've won an Oscar.

That said, prior to the 1960s, there were virtually no outlets for the wealth of black theatrical talent in America. Playwrights writing realistically about the black experience could not get their work produced and even the most successful performers such as Hattie McDaniel and Butterfly McQueen, were confined to playing servants. Disenfranchised artists thus set out to create a theater concentrating primarily on themes of black life. In 1965, playwright Douglas Turner Ward, producer/actor Robert Hooks and theater manager Gerald Krone came together to discuss making these dreams a reality with the Negro Ensemble Company (NEC). The main catalyst for this project was the 1959 production of Lorraine Hansberry's *A Raisin in the Sun*, a gritty and realistic view of black family life in 1950s South Side, Chicago.

The New York Times published a piece in which Ward got to describe the state of black artists in the theater. The Negro Ensemble Company formed officially in 1967, two years after Ward and his peers originally discussed doing something together after funds were raised by the Ford Foundation and a location was secured at the St. Marks Playhouse.

As a child, I was obsessed with the black theatrical experience known as *The Wiz* after seeing excerpts of performances on TV and reading the Playbill mom had brought home after seeing the L.A. staging of the Tony-award-winning musical. I adored Stephanie Mills and all that she represented in the urban remix of *The Wizard of Oz*. When Motown superstars Diana Ross and Michael Jackson were announced to play Dorothy and the Scarecrow respectively in the film adaptation, I was too excited. I continue, even to this day, to get excited every time I happen upon *The Wiz* on TV. I'm that little boy who's just in awe of Diana and the supporting cast inside this whimsical identity questioning tale. The messages in the music, like many words Miss Ross has interpreted over the years, felt like they were coming from my soul. I connected to my own feelings of isolation and difference from my extended family when Dorothy sang Ashford & Simpson's lyrics on "Is This What Feeling Gets?" "Swear to God I don't know the first thing about what they're feeling." Diana whispered, playing her shy version of Dorothy.

I usually start dancing myself in front of the TV when Diana as Dorothy and Michael as the Scarecrow, begin to ease on down the road and pick up their friends the Tin Man and Lion against the backdrop of New York City, eventually arriving in The Emerald City. This was shot in the plaza between the Twin Towers of the World Trade Center, now hauntingly known for their destruction at the hand of terrorists fifteen years later on September 11, 2001. Tony Walton, costume designer for the film curated hundreds of costumes from New York's biggest fashion designers for the dancers who moved en masse under shades of green, red and gold.

I also love when after Dorothy kills the Evilene, her "Winkies" are freed from their weighty, grimy costumes to reveal beautiful black and brown bodies in loincloths and bikinis. It was liberating to see. A breakthrough moment that was electrifying for this seven-year-old.

And though *The Wiz* proved to be initially a box office disappointment, it holds firmly as a classic in the Black community. One reason is that Dorothy's Aunt Em is played by Theresa Merritt, the star of one of my favorite early '70s sitcoms, *That's My Mama*. In the opening scene of the film she's hosting the Thanksgiving dinner at her Harlem home where she lives with her husband and niece, Dorothy. To this day, black families gather to watch *The Wiz* during Thanksgiving and other holidays as it continues to broadcast on networks like BET, TV One, VH1 Soul and Bounce TV.

Mom got to see *Black & Blue* and *Sophisticated Ladies* on Broadway as well, and she took me to see the 1983 musical based on the life and times of African-American singer Doris Troy, *Mama, I Want to Sing*.

Doris Troy was a favorite of the Beatles and had one big hit called "Just One Look." She also sang background on a number of rock & roll hits in the '60s.

Mama's behind-the-scenes mastermind Vy Higginsen, Doris' little sister, is a Harlem-based icon still doing staged work and managing many choirs via her Mama Foundation.

Higginsen's father was a Pentecostal Minister who rejected her sister Doris' ambition to sing. But Doris won Amateur Night at the Apollo Theater and began touring. From day one of being on the road, Doris took Higginsen along. By her late teens, Vy graduated from the Fashion Institute of Technology. Over time, she became the first female advertising executive at *Ebony Magazine*. She later worked as a contributing editor for *Essence* and published and edited her own magazine, *Unique NY*. She then started an iconic decade of work on the radio, hosting shows on WBLS and WWRL as well as reporting for WNBC-TV and The Metro Channel.

Then, with husband-to-be Ken Wydro, she co-wrote and co-produced; *Mama, I Want to Sing!* The show ran for eight years, becoming the longest-running off-Broadway black musical in history. Higginsen played the role of the narrator in the musical. The play was made into a film of the same name in which Higginsen also appeared along with her daughter, Knoelle. "Mama, I Want to Sing! Part 2" and "Born to Sing" rounded out what would become a trilogy of staged pieces centered around different eras of Doris' career. More recently, a musical called *Alive: 55+ and Kickin'* was critically acclaimed and popular to many New Yorkers and tourists once it was featured on the newsmagazine, *60 Minutes*, in 2015.

In 1999, Higginsen founded the Mama Foundation for the Arts. This foundation is a nonprofit organization in Harlem. In 2006, she created Gospel for Teens which offers free gospel music instruction to adolescents through the foundation. The program was featured on *60 Minutes* in a show that won two Emmy Awards in 2012. The show had previously featured a segment on Higginsen tracing her ancestry and learning that she was genetically linked with a white cattle rancher from Missouri. Vy has also become a small business owner with a bestselling hot sauce flying off the shelves at Whole Foods Market. I admire the range of her career as well as her outreaches and her innovation on the stage and off the stage.

Broadway encouraged what media I consumed in a number of ways. I remember that one of the albums I checked out of the library whenever my dad took me to the Oglethorpe Mall branch was *Lena Horne: The Lady and Her Music*. I listened to Lena share her career journey via a 1981 Broadway musical revue written for and starring the American singer and actress. The musical was produced by Michael Frazier and Fred Walker, and the subsequent cast album was produced by Quincy Jones. The show opened on May 12, 1981, and after 333 performances, closed on June 30, 1982 which was Horne's 65th birthday. Horne then toured the show in the U.S. and Canada and performed the work in London and Stockholm in the summer of 1984.

Miss Horne won a special Tony award for this project. Come 2005, she'd be honored alongside Oprah's other Legends, but she was too ill to attend. I got my opportunity to interview her though in 1999 as a contributing editor for *BET Weekend Magazine*. I just had five minutes with Miss Horne to ask her some quick-fire questions about her life and career. I got *Lena Horne: The Lady and Her Music* in ten minutes as she had five additional minutes to spare since we were in a groove. Her beautiful tresses, known over the years in many lengths and styles, were elegantly and simply pulled back and all gray. She wore a simple jacket and blouse combo coupled with a long silk black skirt. I remember her referencing growing up in Brooklyn before there was a Biggie, and it was funny to hear the hip-hop giant's name come out of this industry grandmother's mouth. It was less funny that Biggie had already been dead for two years when Miss Horne and I were talking.

With her extra time, she testified a little bit on how deeply involved she was in the Civil Rights Movement and had been inducted into the International Civil Rights Walk of Fame. She always closed her show with the song "Believe in Yourself" from *The Wiz*, explaining that it took a while for her to believe in herself. The song was quite a helpful affirmation for me as I was growing up.

On her own high from a special Tony Award the year prior for her one-woman show, Lena Horne was chosen to present the award for the best musical of the season. It could have been *Dreamgirls*, *Joseph and the Amazing Technicolor Dreamcoat*, *Nine* or *Pump Boys & Dinettes* but *Nine* won. However, there's no doubt that the cast of *Dreamgirls* knew that they were standing on the shoulders of Lena Horne who'd blazed the trail for all of them to be able to perform in excellence.

As a Miss Ross fan, I'm not supposed to LOVE *Dreamgirls*, the Broadway musical, loosely based on a girl group from the projects. *Dreamgirls* creators, Michael Bennett, Henry Krieger, Tom Eyen and the show's producers deny any connections between the musical's plot and the Supremes life stories. However, the similarities between the show and actual life events within the Supremes led many to believe that the creators did actually base the musical's story on the group. It's widely believed the producers denied connections in order to avoid lawsuits from Motown, Berry Gordy and the Supremes. Still, original Supreme Mary Wilson loved *Dreamgirls* so much that she named her first autobiography after the musical, *Dreamgirl: My Life as a Supreme*. Diana Ross performed "Family" from Act I in her historic free concert in New York City's Central Park in July, 1983. Though the Deena character mirrors Diana Ross, actress/vocalist Sheryl Lee Ralph stated that she wasn't trying to imitate Ross but rather portray Deena in a similar yet distinct style.

So, the real-world tale is legendary, but I'll recap: Diana Ross, Mary Wilson and Florence Ballard were The Supremes. By 1967, they were renamed Diana Ross and The Supremes. Berry Gordy's *Motown the Musical* and other biographical projects recall the time that Florence was growing weary of the spotlight and always landing on Miss Ross for press, leads on songs and perhaps, the straw that broke the camel's back, the affections of Motown founder Berry Gordy. That perfect storm of influence increased the stakes and how much of the machine would lean on Miss Ross to produce top-notch performances every time. At the same time, they all say Florence grew more and more disgruntled. She eventually left the group and started her solo career. Ballard was replaced by Cindy Birdsong who was a member of the quartet, Patti LaBelle & the Bluebelles. Many years later all of these moves would produce bad blood between Mary Wilson and Diana Ross. It turns out that there was no love-loss between Patti LaBelle and Miss Ross either as Patti didn't appreciate Motown snatching her group member.

Florence's dramatic exit would never get the luxury of the Act 2 that her doppelganger, Effie White, gets in Dreamgirls. Florence died penniless on welfare in 1976 of what some describe as a "broken heart." Effie fell from grace in Dreamgirls but got the luxury of a comeback and a reconciliation with her group, Deena Jones & the Dreams.

What stands out in the creative license of this non-Supremes story is that unlike Florence Ballard who died in the mid-1970s of a heart attack, Effie White breaks through her troubles to come back as a solo artist and actually reunites with her bandmates.

I've had the chance to know the original Dreamgirls, Sheryl Lee Ralph and Loretta Devine over the years. In my book and by most estimates, these women are Broadway, as well as, entertainment royalty and they are still workhorses. Plus, the *Dreamgirls* soundtrack made me fall in love with Jennifer Holliday. On any given night, Holliday would bring sold-out audiences of enthusiastic Broadway patrons to their feet when she'd close out Act 1. Before *American Idol* bred, Jennifer Hudson took home an Academy Award for playing the big screen version of Effie White. The role was created for the Broadway stage and standing ovations by Holliday who belted out her signature, guttural ballad "And I Am Telling You I'm Not Going" with a last line no one has been able to mimic in quite the same way since. Holliday still performs the song on command! Last year she did the Apollo Amateur Night staple on ABC talk show *The View* as she joined, moderator, Whoopi Goldberg's lip sync of the classic karaoke selection. Her live and bombastic vocals made many believe it was still December 20, 1981, when *Dreamgirls* opened. With her stellar career of recording hits, from torch ballads to dance chart-toppers, to an array of gospel tunes including a 1985 recording of Duke Ellington's "Come Sunday" that garnered her a Grammy for Best Inspirational Performance, Holliday has attracted global bookings that spotlight her special brand of performance. This includes back-to-back Democratic national conventions in 1984 and '88. Primarily known for her stage work, Holliday was also cast as Lisa Knowles on the hit show "Ally McBeal" in 1997. Through all of those years, she'd also do select Broadway fare such as Big Mama Morton in *Chicago* and Teen Angel in *Grease*. She returned to critical acclaim on Broadway in October 2016 by jumping into a fourteen-week limited engagement of the revival of *The Color Purple*. She played sexy cabaret singer Shug Avery, a role originated in the revival by Grammy winner Hudson and later taken up by fellow Tony and Grammy winner Heather Headley.

There are Broadway shows that allow me to escape into a musical wonderland, like *The Wiz*, or to reflect with creative license on someone else's history or a moment in time, like *Lena Horne: The Lady & Her Music* or *Dreamgirls*. Then came *Rent* which put a mirror on the AIDS crisis.

When I first saw *Rent* after I moved to New York City, it gave my own need to be liberated and come out as gay as it captured the dark side of urban life during the '80s when America was trying to get a handle on AIDS. In all of its grit, the rock musical *Rent* provides an urban tale of poor struggling artists in the East Village of New York City during the '80s when HIV/AIDS loomed and one-by-one, we began to lose loved ones. Additionally, because of the book and the music, Jonathan Larson provides a soundtrack that has stood the test of time. The song "Seasons of Love" is a classic. In the lyric, the cast sings "Five hundred twenty-five thousand six hundred minutes," a year's worth.

AIDS was something to be afraid of during this time. The disease, along with other STDs, seemed like it was affecting the gay community in higher numbers. Especially LGBTQ communities of color. I had the sense in all my sexual pursuits that "wrapping it up," keeping matters safe and sexy was the only way to go because the disease was out there. And it's why I didn't fully explore a man until I was almost out of college. My fear stemmed from two cousins, one on each side, who passed away from AIDS. Their sexualities weren't the question, but the stigma spoke volumes and you could hear a pin drop on any further discussions from relatives on the respective losses. So, I had a lot of suppressed fear stemming from how those losses impacted our families.

With such circumstances lingering, I couldn't see my truth as a lifestyle for several years after I graduated college. I had to grow the courage to come out.

By 2001, I had a mantra that I would tell my close, platonic friends who were girls and I'd come out to my gay guy friends as well. I looked forward to the day when I could actually go on a date with a man to one of these Broadway shows for which I got comps. Starting in 2001, I started an on-again/off-again romance with a man I'd met in 1999 at my girlfriend Michelle's Chelsea pad. At least Kodjoe says that's when we met. He was with someone at the time anyway. Though I wasn't involved with anyone, I wasn't looking in the direction of breaking up a happy home. Fast forward a year or so and we reconnected via Michelle and our same crew of friends on a fun night out in the city. Coincidentally, as I continued to dabble in performance on the sidelines when I moved to New York City, our first date would be after a cabaret performance I did at The Duplex in the Village. He really enjoyed the show and afterwards, he took me out for a bite at a nearby restaurant. In ordering a salad, I asked for no onions. "Should I get no onions as well?" Kodjoe asked, giving me the first sign that we were going to have our first kiss later. He didn't get the onions.

At this time, he was available. My eyes were open and as quickly as I write this, we decided to date. Soon we were wining and dining and going out to see Broadway shows. As mutual *Dreamgirls* fans, we were too excited to go see Sheryl Lee Ralph in *Thoroughly Modern Millie* in which Whoopi Goldberg was one of the producers.

Kodjoe and I were going to take it slow since he'd just gotten out of the aforementioned situation, but we were poised to date indeed, and beyond. We loved Houston's and spoke of many legends over its famous spinach and artichoke dip. We also engaged enthusiastically with our divas and proclaimed it by going to see as many of them as we could including Madonna and Tina Turner. By Christmas 2001, my new client Oprah Winfrey invited me and a guest to her winter holiday party in Chicago, so we'd upgraded our grown folks relationship to Chicago travel and destination date nights. It was bliss.

Once Kodjoe got a gig in Nashville and the long distance tore us apart. We continued to be fond of each other but the due diligence that we each did to please our respective employers made for no time to maintain a relationship from across state lines. Because Kodjoe felt his gig away would be just a couple of years, he asked if we could pick our relationship up pending his return.

I agreed but sassily retorted, "Call first. I might have company!"

I didn't. A couple of years later he returned to New York City ready to pick up where we left off and so we did which resulted in a year's worth of romance, date nights, support and talk of a future together. As he came from a traditional Ghanaian-American household, being gay was not easy for Kodjoe. He was gay, and his parents knew. They didn't engage him on anything around his orientation, even his prior love interest, he'd tell me. But Kodjoe wanted to break through the challenge and round out what love looked like on him with me. We had plans on how we'd do that. The following year, one thing we committed to do was attend his first cousin Boris's wedding in Germany to actress Nicole Ari Parker with their first baby on the way. Kodjoe was excited that this would be our "coming out" to the extended family including cousins, aunts and uncles. First things first, he wanted me to meet his sisters' children, the nieces and nephew who were the light of his life. Much like my nephew Herman was to me. He adored them and wanted them to meet "Uncle Patrick." And sure enough, I fell in love with the kids as we all gathered for ice skating and bowling at Chelsea Pier, sealing the evening with a kiss.

A nightmare awakened me the next day as I saw Kodjoe's number come through my caller ID on what would be Easter Sunday morning. With a smile, I answered the phone. "Hey babe." I said, awaiting what was normally an exhale and a giggle when he'd call, and I answered. The voice on the other end was not Kodjoe. It was the youngest of his two sisters, Ofie, letting me know that Kodjoe passed away in his sleep overnight. He'd dropped the kids off at his parents' home in Queens and decided to stay the night before returning to his apartment in Stamford, Connecticut. They found him later that morning with a smile on his face.

I was paralyzed, unable to move for about a half hour. Eventually I found the strength to get an email out to as many as I could to inform our friends and New York City family. I truly wondered how I could have found love, gotten clarity that I was loved back and in one fell swoop, lost it all. One-by-one my New York City fam came to the rescue.

To gay couples, premature death isn't far fetched. When you meet a potential love interest, the worry, certainly in my twenties and thirties was, "Does he have HIV? Is he going to die?"

Well, Kodjoe died in his sleep at 37 but in a Broadway twist, he wasn't ravaged by AIDS. His heart stopped. Though he had a history of heart complications, things were really looking up with his health as he had a procedure that prevented those episodes in which the heart beats really rapidly. And I was right there alongside him as we continued to grow closer and happier with ourselves and each other, then he died, and I was devastated.

Years later, I'd forgotten just how devastated I was when I met Ant on the opening night of Broadway's, *The Color Purple*. It was December 1, 2005, coincidentally World AIDS Day.

The next year, my friend LaChanze won the Tony Award for Best Performance by a Leading Actress in a Musical in 2006 for her role in *Purple*. While LaChanze was eight months pregnant with her second child, her husband, securities trader Calvin Gooding, was killed in the September 11, 2001 attacks. He was working at Cantor Fitzgerald in Tower One of the World Trade Center.

Anthony was covering the red carpet for STARZ, a Denver based cable channel. Opening night and Oprah's much-anticipated appearance next door in the Ed Sullivan Theater made this my freelance assignment from Harpo. He and his associate producer Sabrina would joke later that they were covering the red carpet and I was on the red carpet because Oprah's cameras got front-line access. Ant was a producer, easy on the eyes, smart and an Air Force brat. When I talked to him at a party held later, I wasn't sure he was gay. He was friendly enough but seemed much too shy for my taste. Still, he stayed engaged with our conversation and once we all left the party and proceeded to the after party at the New York Public Library, I mentioned the lion statues in front of the 5th Avenue entrance were muses for the Lion's first scene in the movie version of *The Wiz*. Ant was amused. We then went to Luke & Leroy in the Village to join other LGBTQ men of color for our continued fete. Ant mentioned he'd been to the place the last time he visited New York from Denver and I had my answer about his sexuality.

We started out long-distance, making monthly commitments to see each other and not one month passing without us honoring that agreement. Then, by 2006, he moved here, and we began the next on-going chapter of our life and love while also coping with huge adjustments, breakdowns and challenges. We've been with each other through many amazing experiences from Broadway to Manila to Maui, and some challenging times such as continuing to struggle with the loss of his dad, who passed away in June 2016, as well as health concerns.

Broadway brings the humanity. Sometimes the humanity comes to Broadway and produces love. Ant and I are a living testimonial to that and have continued to enjoy myriad versions of *The Color Purple* over the years. It's our show and it's our life, marked by meeting on opening night. We were with LaChanze the night she won the Tony Awards in June 2006. As she would marry again in the wake of her tragic loss, her second husband would happen to be from Ghana. Ant and I attended the wedding and it seemed in some ways, because of all of the Ghanaian traditions that were appointed throughout the ceremony and reception, a passing of the torch from Kodjoe to my new love Anthony.

All kinds of Broadway and Off-Broadway fare comprise my many date nights with Ant. It's so uplifting and inspiring for us whenever we see a new show or go back to re-experience an older show with a new cast or a new director's vision.

In January 2008, Anthony and I got in a huge argument, the content of which I forget, but the heat of the moment begged the question "Should we break up?" Neither of us was equipped at the time to give an answer. We went on about our respective days but were scheduled to reconnect later for the final run of the first version of *The Color Purple* on Broadway. By this time, Chaka Khan was playing Sophia and BeBe Winans was Harpo. This would be Ant's and my sixth time seeing the show. In the wake of our earlier argument, we were still tense. As we witnessed the musical one more time, taking us on a ride that reminds us to be grateful for the beauty and love we have right before our eyes like the color of purple in a field, tears rolled down our eyes.

Ant and I got ourselves together and embraced which was followed by apologies. As the cast was singing the final bars to the reprise of the show's theme song, Ant and I were healed. That's what *The Color Purple* did for us. That's what Broadway and the many women I admire on those stages and creating those shows do for me.

SCRAPBOOK

Sheryl Lee Ralph's, Deena on Broadway in Dreamgirls was a break-out role in the early '80s. She continued to be booked late into the '90s, most notably as Brandy's stepmom Dee in Moesha. Her most recent role is in the second season of TNT's **Claws** alongside Niecy Nash. She's also had recurring roles on **MacGyver**, BET's **The Quad**, and Netflix's comedy film **Step Sisters**.

I've been a fan of Sheryl Lee Ralph's since her guest starring role on **Good Times** in which she declared to her boyfriend, J.J., "The night air is murder on lip gloss!" While in Los Angeles in October 2009, Ant and I attended Sheryl Lee Ralph's annual AIDS awareness fundraiser Divas: Simply Singing.

In early June 2015, I was thrilled to be among an industry few who got to come out to an intimate **The Color Purple** cocktail party at The Cafe at Pier 59 to introduce its Broadway stars, Jennifer Hudson, Cynthia Erivo and Danielle Brooks. Though the show's leads were meeting for the first time on this day, they told me their chemistry felt instant.

I'd known Lachanze since 2001, but she became a fairy god-sister on December 1, 2005 as she opened as Miss Celie in Broadway's **The Color Purple**. I met my partner Ant that night. Since then, Ant and I have supported all of Lachanze's showcases around town from periodic sets at 54 Below Supper Club and special American Songbook performances at Jazz at Lincoln Center. Her latest Broadway turn is as one of the three Donna Summers in Broadway musical **Summer: The Donna Summer Musical.**

Motown the Musical opened April 2013. It was great to catch up with Tony-award-winning actress Lachanze at the Roseland Ballroom after party.

Lachanze performed a tribute to Diana Ross at 54 Below in the Spring and Summer of 2013. I rushed backstage to tell her she did a great job!

I hosted The All-Star Karaoke at a Native Restaurant in Harlem from 2010 until 2011. One of our Broadway favorites, Brenda Braxton who was known for a long run in Broadway's **Chicago**, came by to offer our enthusiastic crowd some free tickets to see her show.

In October 2015, Lillias White starred in Billy Porter's play, **While I Yet Live**. I went to one of the previews and surprised Lillias backstage after the show which ran as a limited engagement at Primary Stages at The Duke on 42nd Street.

WOMEN ON BROADWAY | 93

In June 2012, Project1Voice Producers asked me to share the spotlight with Tony Award Winners: Lillias White, Chuck Cooper and Adriane Lenox for a soul stirring, staged reading of James Baldwin's, The Amen Corner at John Jay College's Gerald W. Lynch Theater. I was one of the media insiders cast as a stage narrator providing Adriane and the rest of the leads and supporting cast their cues to deliver their lines.

After the first preview of Broadways **A Streetcar Named Desire** in March 2012, I met actress Tonya Pinkins at Bourbon Street where many dine before or after a show. The veteran Broadway actress won a Tony for **Jelly's Last Jam** in 1992. In 2003, she originated the lead in Tony Kushner's 2003 Broadway musical **Caroline, or Change**.

In November 2015, Tonya Pinkins invited me to a preview of her Off-Broadway play **Mother Courage and Her Children** at Classic Stage Company. She was to open January 2016 but vacated the show due to creative differences with the producers. The preview we saw was spectacular.

In 2014 when Audra McDonald played Billie Holiday in Lady Day at Emerson's Bar & Grill, she became the first performer to win in all four performance categories. Additionally, she's won the most Tonys. She'd won prior for The Gershwin's' **Porgy and Bess, A Raisin in the Sun, Ragtime, Master Class,** and **Carousel**. She's also done TV including **Private Practice** and **Annie and Wit.**

May 2015, I'm here in front of the Circle in the Square Theatre after seeing Audra McDonald in her Tony-award-winning turn as Billie Holiday in **Lady Day at Emerson's Bar and Grill.** I included Audra in my monthly Broadway round-up for Arise Entertainment 360.

Frenchie Davis, who performed in **Rent** and as Effie on a traveling production of **Dreamgirls** was among the DIVAS who performed for Sheryl Lee Ralph's **Diva: Simply Singing** AIDS Foundation event in October 2009. This is where I met the former **American Idol** contestant then known for abruptly leaving the second season of the show. We have had the chance to bond over the years. She's straight-forward, passionate and always good for a great debate! Social media has provided her another platform for her own brand of "what the f***!" And she continues to book great stages globally.

As a featured performer in Danai Gurira play **Eclipsed**, Saycon Sengbloh was nominated for a Tony and won a Drama Desk Award in 2016.

Here we are in September 2013 at Edwing D'Angelo's New York Fashion Week show. Saycon was preparing to star in **Motown the Musical** as Martha Reeves.

Saycon and I at New York's legendary Sardi's Restaurant in May 2014, toasting **Holler If Ya Hear Me**, a musical based on the poetry and lyrics of Tupac Shakur. The show was directed by Kenny Leon, who directed me in Morehouse College and Clark Atlanta University productions in the '90s.

chapter 6

Black Beauties

Throughout the '70s, my mom tuned in to the Miss America pageant every year, and I sat right in front of the TV and watched it with her, since it was usually on a Saturday night. Adults told me that the pageants were designed to promote healthy competition among women and build the character of the many young ladies who competed. As a little boy who loved glamour and entertainment, at first I simply enjoyed the sparkling visuals of these contests. It wasn't until the 1980s that I awakened to the primarily white aesthetic of beauty being presented and began to hear the feminists of the time speak of how the pageant system, especially the swimsuit competition, objectified women. So when a black woman won the Miss America crown in 1983, it meant something.

On the night of the pageant, I fell in love with Vanessa Williams, the striking five-foot-six, 20-year-old Miss New York. My mom was sprawled across the couch and I was lying on my stomach on the floor, captivated by Williams' grace and beauty. When she sang "Happy Days Are Here Again," I knew she would take home the crown and become a great talent, even though Suzette Charles, Miss New Jersey, gave a stellar performance of "Kiss Me in the Rain." Williams was so poised, and her voice so pristine and powerful, with the old-fashioned glamour and elegance of a Lena Horne or Nancy Wilson. Not only was Williams crowned Miss America 1984, becoming the first black woman to hold the title, but she and Charles, the first runner-up, were also the first black women to win their state pageants. But in the following July, Williams was forced to resign after nude photos of her surfaced. I was heartbroken when Williams returned the rhinestone-studded crown and it passed to Charles instead.

But the green-eyed, brown-haired beauty didn't give up. Vanessa Williams' manager, Ramon Hervey, came to the rescue, setting up a series of TV, stage, and recording projects. They got married and had three kids: two girls and a boy. One of their daughters is a member of neo-soul sensation Lion Babe.

Vanessa Williams' success was sealed when she released her much-anticipated debut album *The Right Stuff*. I immediately put the recording into heavy rotation, as the title track and first single was quite the dance ditty. The spectacular music video for "The Right Stuff," filmed in Baton Rouge and New Orleans, showcased Williams' style, dancing talent, and dramatic appeal as she pursued the leading man, the beginning of volumes of gorgeous iconography with a range of looks and imagery that further extended her beauty into the stratosphere throughout the '80s and '90s. The follow-up single "(He's Got) The Look" and ballads "Dreamin'" and "Darlin' I" also became R&B and pop hits. The album eventually went gold and earned Williams three Grammy nominations.

I continued to follow Vanessa Williams' every appearance and absolutely adored her 1991 second album, *The Comfort Zone*, which included the sultry title track, the single "Running Back to You," and her Grammy-nominated hit ballad "Save the Best for Last." The album *The Sweetest Days* came out right after my mom passed away in 1994, so its moody swing, exemplified by Babyface's bossa nova-style "Betcha Never," was like a touch of salve in my time of grief.

In early 1995, I took a special trip to New York to see Vanessa Williams' Broadway debut in *Kiss of the Spider Woman*, after which she greeted my childhood friend Ernest and me in her dressing room. Her face was free of makeup but still beautiful, if unrecognizable, and she was sporting a simple gray turtleneck as she unpretentiously invited us into the tiny space with a small mirror framed with high-frequency stage lights. After a few minutes of awkward small talk, we gushed over her performance, got her to sign our playbills, and took a quick picture with her in that wonderful encounter with one of my favorite divas.

In addition to more recording and stage performances, Vanessa Williams has done a lot of TV and film work. She received an NAACP Image Award for Outstanding Actress in a Motion Picture for her role in the 1997 film *Soul Food*. Williams' best-known television role was on *Ugly Betty* from 2006 to 2010, which brought her two Emmy nominations. She also did a stint on *Desperate Housewives* from 2010 to 2012.

Vanessa Williams' journey went full circle when she returned to the Miss America stage on September 13, 2015, for the Miss America 2016 pageant, serving as the head judge and performing "Oh How the Years Go By." The pageant began with Miss America CEO Sam Haskell's statement to Williams that although "none of us currently in the organization were involved then, on behalf of today's organization, I want to apologize to you and to your mother, Miss Helen Williams. I want to apologize for anything that was said or done that made you feel any less the Miss America you are and the Miss America you always will be." Williams has continued to be a major draw across platforms as the most successful Miss America of all time, an inspirational example for anyone who hits rock bottom.

Seven other black women have worn the Miss America crown after Vanessa Williams, including Suzette Charles. The way had been paved for them by Cheryl Brown, Miss Iowa, the first black contestant to compete in the national pageant in 1970. Over the span of nearly half a century, black women from sea to shining sea have represented states from Dixie to Delaware. Black women have been especially adept at parlaying the opportunities intrinsic to wearing the crown into considerable success in a variety of professions, such as entertainment, journalism, and politics. Debbye Turner, for instance, was pursuing a doctorate in veterinary medicine when she won, Marjorie Vincent a Duke University law degree.

Black models, the other icons of beauty, have always held a certain allure. Ever since the slogan "Black Is Beautiful" was coined in the '60s, we've endeavored to embrace it and seen good results with the success of models like Beverly Johnson, Iman, Naomi Campbell, Tyra Banks, and Veronica Webb. Aside perhaps from actresses, models have confronted the devaluation of black beauty more than any other professionals. There have been reports of black models being rejected, ignored, or worse, simply replaced by white models in blackface.

But these women were resilient. Otherwise, black models simply wouldn't have been hired. In the 1970s, they created their own makeup products because makeup artists often didn't have any foundations for darker skin tones. Models also had to compensate for technicians who weren't familiar with black hair, which led to the boom in straight hair extensions, a texture stylists knew how to work with. Even the great Naomi Campbell has reported that when she entered the modeling business, she had to lug styling kits to shoots.

Still, black models persevered, just like their peers in other industries. In 1974, Beverly Johnson became the first black model to appear on the cover of *Vogue* magazine, which made such an impact that every major fashion magazine ran a woman of color on the cover within a year.

One of the world's most recognizable faces for two decades, Iman was discovered by a photographer while at Nairobi University, eventually moving to the United States to begin a modeling career. Her first assignment for *Vogue* in 1976 was revolutionary in that she was Somalian with beautiful dark skin, whereas Beverly Johnson had European features and lighter skin. Iman soon landed some of the most prestigious magazine covers, establishing herself as a supermodel with her tall carriage, elongated neck and torso, slim body, and copper skin tone. I enjoyed seeing her in the pages of *Ebony* and all of the fashion magazines. Iman was also a muse for many prominent fashion designers, including Halston, Gianni Versace, Calvin Klein, Issey

Miyake, and Donna Karan. She was very close to Yves Saint-Laurent, who once described her as his "dream woman."

As a model-muse, Iman was often an integral part of the creative process. It's no surprise, then, that after almost two decades of modeling, she started her own cosmetics firm in 1994, focusing on difficult-to-find shades for women of all colors. By 2010, IMAN Cosmetics was a $25-million business. Iman also has a Home Shopping Network line and dabbled in TV and film, including *Star Trek VI: The Undiscovered Country* and Michael Jackson's music video for "Remember the Time."

In 1996, Tyra Banks made waves as the first black woman to be featured on the cover of *Sports Illustrated* magazine's annual swimsuit issue. Her appearance on the cover alongside Argentine model Valeria Mazza turned the 22-year-old Banks into a household name. The following year, she was featured again on the cover of the swimsuit issue, this time appearing solo.

Since then, black models like Jessica White, Quiana Grant, Chanel Iman, and Damaris Lewis have been shown on the pages inside the popular swimsuit issue, with Beyoncé as the next black woman to grace the cover in 2007. Nonetheless, as of this writing Tyra Banks remains the only black model to make it onto the cover over a period of 52 years. Iman and activist Bethann Hardison, who once ran the New York City studio for fashion designer Stephen Burrows and was the maid of honor at the wedding of Iman and English rock musician David Bowie, are working to change that through their campaign, "Actually She Can," which advocates for greater diversity on the runway but focuses on female mentorship for women in the fashion and modeling industries.

Tyra Banks is one of my favorites to watch and study. She created an industry within an industry with the reality show *America's Next Top Model*, an interactive competition in which a number of aspiring models compete for the title of America's Next Top Model and a chance to begin a career in the modeling industry. Each season starts with a dozen contestants who are judged every week on their overall appearances while participating in special challenges. Every season, the semi-finalists also take a trip to an international destination. Banks' ability to instruct contestants is absolutely magical. I use her tricks as well, including "smizing," which means smiling with your eyes, not just your lips. My partner, Ant, and I still love the show in all of its incarnations.

In addition to creating and executive producing the reality show, Tyra Banks has become a force in pop culture responsible for introducing more models of color onto the scene, including Eva Marcille, Toccara Jones, and Yaya DaCosta, who played the title role in the Lifetime movie about Whitney Houston. Banks has also become the host of *America's Got Talent* after having her own talk show. This mogul has inspired a generation of female entrepreneurs to go for their dreams—in color.

SCRAPBOOK

When I met Toni Seawright in the mid-'90s, I already knew her as the first black woman to become Miss Mississippi and as the fourth runner-up in the 1988 Miss America pageant. Then I met her again in the late '90s after moving to New York City. As it turned out, she'd been spending much of that decade singing with a number of artists, including Teena Marie, Freddie Jackson, Tony Terry, RuPaul, Shaggy, and Laura Branigan. Seawright also starred alongside Stephanie Mills and Andre De Shields in the musical **The Wiz**. She currently writes and produces material for her two sons, Qaasim Middleton, who was a finalist on Season 14 of **American Idol**, and Khalil Middleton—both of whom starred alongside me in the film **Steps**, executive produced by Shaquille O'Neal.

In June 2014, I was at singer-songwriter Toni Seawright's fiftieth birthday party, where I led a tribute to Michael Jackson, who died on the same day.

I've loved Vanessa Williams from her Miss America days, to her first album, **The Right Stuff**, to her more recent bookings, such as **Daytime Divas**. Even though I wasn't living in New York City yet, I was such a big fan that I arranged for tickets to her 1995 Broadway debut in **Kiss of the Spider Woman** and a backstage visit.

I met with Vanessa Williams backstage after her Broadway show **After Midnight** in November 2016.

In January 2013, Vanessa Williams was honored by the Dance Theatre of Harlem, along with her daughter, who is now a recording artist and performer in the group Lion Babe.

Iman is a legend not even supermodel Naomi Campbell would dare disrespect. When I was producing her interview with Iman, Campbell was hesitant to ask if she'd had a nip and tuck. I suggested framing it, "Iman, I know black doesn't crack, but would you ever do plastic surgery?" Campbell nodded and followed my advice. Iman appreciated the clever wording.

I interviewed Iman about her eponymous cosmetics line in January 2016, less than a month before her husband, David Bowie, passed away.

Supermodel Veronica Webb and I went to a promotional party at Vivid Lounge in September 2010 for the raising of a Times Square billboard for Hair Rules, the innovative hair care salon founded by supermodel Kara Young and celebrity stylist Dickey.

I met Beverly Johnson in 1994 just after my mother passed away. A longtime friend of mine, fashion producer Carl Nelson, wanted to promote Johnson's appearance on **Good Day Atlanta** at his iconic Drums Along the Hudson annual outdoor family festival, which I've hosted for the last decade. We booked her, of course, and I made another best friend.

In March 2012, Beverly Johnson was in New York City, promoting her Oprah Winfrey Network show **Beverly's Full House** and a new skin product. She invited some members of the press to join her for breakfast at the Opia Hotel.

Toccara Jones gained notoriety as a contestant in the third season of the UPN series **America's Next Top Model**, where she finished in seventh place. She and I had a ball at the Edwing D'Angelo fashion show during Fashion Week on September 12, 2013.

To kick off fall 2010, Toccara Jones hosted a cocktail party in New York City.

Yaya DaCosta was the runner-up in the third season of **America's Next Top Model**. In 2015, she began starring in the NBC medical drama **Chicago Med**. Her role as Whitney Houston in a Lifetime movie also brought her notoriety, as did her role opposite David Oyelowo in **Lee Daniel's The Butler**.

In February 2011, I spotted Yaya DaCosta at Tyler Perry's **For Colored Girls** premiere and after-party in New York.

In September 2013, Yaya DaCosta and I were at an Oscars campaign luncheon at Brasserie Ruhlmann in Rockefeller Plaza for the NAACP Image Award-winning documentary about Angela Davis, **Free Angela and All Political Prisoners**, produced by my friend Sidra Smith.

chapter 7

Famous Families

One of the most talked about hit television shows of the 2010s has been *Empire*, the story of a black family running a music label. The dynasty began with the musical talent of the father and business acumen of the mother. A couple of decades later, it is the sons' musical prowess the company's future hinges on. It's surprising that it took so long for this concept to make its way to the screen as it has all the ingredients for a good show including beauty, music, friction, decadence, and the list goes on.

One of *Empire*'s stars grew up in one of the more extreme instances of this. Far from being impossible, part of the plot is actually realistic. Professional/industry surveys have long established that the majority of jobs are obtained by networks, based on who one knows, and it's hard to know someone better than your family. It might be known as nepotism elsewhere but in the entertainment business, passing on the family business is called a musical or acting "dynasty" because you're building a legacy.

One of *Empire*'s stars has shared this seemingly idyllic experience. Jussie Smollett, who plays Jamal, the most talented member of the Lyon hip-hop dynasty, actually began his career co-starring with his five siblings in the short-lived 1994 ABC sitcom, *On Our Own*. Most of the family-based cast have gone on to other careers while the most accomplished actor of the group, sister Jurnee Smollett-Bell, made waves at the age of 10 in the 1997 film *Eve's Bayou*. She has since co-starred with Denzel Washington in *The Great Debaters*, playing a member of all-black Wiley College's 1935 debate team which won the national championship. She later played the lead in *Underground*, a drama about a group of slaves who try to escape from their Georgia plantation.

The two stars paint an idyllic picture of growing up like a modern-day version of the black von Trapps. The kids entertained themselves with dramatic readings and dance-offs. Their mother, Janet, was the family's acting coach and old movies kept them entertained.

My family has close enough ties that if we were to build an entertainment dynasty, it could stand impressively. However, I chose a professional route different from everybody else in my family.

There's something about sisters in the business that intrigues me. As much as my parents taught me, my siblings taught me how to navigate the world. It was with them that I learned how to deal with conflict, share responsibilities and work through being competitive, envious and mean. They were my protectors and best friends. I often observe the same dynamics for the sisters I know in the business. In the best cases, they give each other courage and confidence.

Often, my siblings were that for me. But we've gone in directions too different to collaborate like the Emotions or Clark Sisters did to massive success. My sister Janice has been married for more than two decades but has no kids. She was a legal secretary for many years and is now a county judge's assistant. She doesn't sing, though she can hold a tune and sometimes joins the church choir.

My brother Herman can sing. However, he never chose a performance career per se but could have easily been a sports broadcaster. As children in the mid '70s, he and I did start a singing group during our Air Force days in San Bernadino, California. We were PHD Incorporated, as in Patrick, Herman and Derrick. Derrick and his family lived down the street from us in base housing. After Derrick's father got relocated to another country, another Derrick came into town and we did a Florence-Ballard-Supremes-style replacement a la Cindy Birdsong.

My lead song was often, "Easy" by the Commodores. I also had the high part on "Boogie Fever." My brother Herman regularly did, "Let's Just Kiss & Say Goodbye." We were good. Or thought we were, with Mom's styling and my sister's choreography. So, I guess we tried to work together. Still, our lives moved in different directions.

What I don't know is what it would have looked like had my brother and I taken our talent on the road for the world to see like so many family units. Units who have experienced great success, from Chicago's Hutchinson sisters, who we got to know as the angelic voices behind the disco hit, "Best of My Love" and Earth, Wind, & Fire's, "Boogie Wonderland," or The Clark Sisters, Detroit's new generation of Arethas who also took their sound international and to the clubs. Their biggest hit was, "You Brought The Sunshine In My Life," which has a Stevie Wonder "Master Blaster" feel to it.

Debbie Allen and Phylicia Rashad are the ultimate role models for siblings working together, apart, and nurturing the next generation. After attending Howard University together, the radiant sisters embarked on careers on Broadway. Debbie is perhaps best known for her work on the 1982 musical-drama television series *Fame*, where she portrayed dance teacher Lydia Grant, and served as the series' principal choreographer. Once *Fame* syndicated, I watched it every afternoon when I got home from school. I also bought all of the albums, featuring their show performances and the cast's live concerts.

Debbie still acts in front of the camera, more recently as Catherine Avery on *Grey's Anatomy*. And I still hold dear one of her earlier television appearances in the TV sitcom *Good Times*, a two-part episode titled, "J.J.'s Fiancée'." Debbie plays J.J.'s drug-addicted betrothed, Diana.

As a director, we've witnessed Debbie's expertise from *A Different World* to *Scandal*. I had the chance to cover the first rehearsal of her all-black cast of *Cat on a Hot Tin Roof* on Broadway in 2008. Phylicia Rashad and James Earl Jones led the pack. I felt like I was looking at Lydia Grant from *Fame* as she commanded the thespians. Lydia was a choreographer and Debbie was the boss.

Debbie is married to former NBA player Norm Nixon, the two have a son and a daughter. Daughter Vivian, while still in her final year of the Ailey/Fordham BFA Program in Dance, was cast as Kalinda by Hot Feet's conceiver/director/choreographer, Maurice Hines in 2007. Hot Feet follows the classic storyline of *The Red Shoes* with a '70s funk facelift.

Phylicia became an '80s icon playing the role of lawyer-mother-wife, Clair Huxtable, on *The Cosby Show*. Since the series went off the air in 1992, Rashad has become a top Broadway actress, winning a Tony Award for her role in the 2004 revival of *A Raisin in the Sun*.

Like Debbie, her daughter Condola, with pro football player and sportscaster Ahmad Rashad, is a chip off the old block. She graduated from the California Institute of the Arts in 2008. Her acting has been lauded, including Tony nominations for her Broadway performances in *Stick Fly* and *The Trip to Bountiful*. She starred as the lead in Broadway's 2013 run of Shakespeare's *Romeo and Juliet*. As I spent 2013 through 2016 doing recurring theater reviews for COZI-TV and Arise Entertainment 360, on Nigerian-based, global network Arise News, I always enjoyed including Condola's family ties in my coverage.

On television, Condola played Shelby in a remake of *Steel Magnolias*. In the original film, the role was played by Julia Roberts. She's also guest-starred on *The Good Wife* and *Law & Order: Criminal Intent*.

Though Debbie and Phylicia have done small projects together, they've largely chartered independent professional careers. They've always presented a united front, and never have we seen a rift. Now, their daughters support each other just the same, as first cousins.

Tia and Tamera Mowry are another great example of making blood count for something. These two had their greatest success to date from 1994-99 staring as twins on the hit comedy series *Sister, Sister*. They also found success in 2011 with the reality show *Tia & Tamera*.

From 2006 until 2012, Tia gained fame portraying medical student Melanie Barnett on the CW/BET comedy-drama series *The Game*. Tamera has booked her share of acting parts as well but is now seen daily as one of the hosts of *The Real* talk show along with Adrienne Bailon, Jeannie Mai and Loni Love, which premiered on July 15, 2013. Both twins appreciate their independence, but say they aren't afraid to work together as they understand the magic they have as sisters.

The Braxton sisters may know they have something special, but it includes their friction and rivalries. Not all siblings get along splendidly.

We see that on the reality show *The Braxton Family Values*. Superstar Toni Braxton decided to share the spotlight with lesser known sisters Traci, Towanda, Tina and breakout star Tamar. Since Toni got her La Face deal, she's brought her sisters along, first as background singers. She then hooked them up with a short-lived recording contract which saw the release of the 1996 album *So Many Ways*. Years later, the show picked them up as background singers for Toni but all aiming to do their own thing.

Tamar made the biggest splash, landing a few hit songs that included, "Love & War." She also had a successful Emmy-nominated run as a co-host on *The Real*, but she was fired, setting off a dramatic development that would lead up to a pending divorce from Tamar and her husband/manager Vince.

What shows up though is that these women love each-other and, through their hurts and music, they always come together and try to be harmonious.

Seeing them has made me wonder what it would've been like to more intimately witness, with reality TV cameras, '70s singing groups like Sister Sledge and the Pointer Sisters in which rivalries and conflicts have been openly discussed. I have a peripheral reflection of the Pointer Sisters during that era, perhaps the most impactful impression being one from 1976 as they were the voices on "Pinball Number Count," an animated video in which the siblings sing a count from one to twelve on *Sesame Street*. I knew how to count by then but loved the song anyway. "Yes, We Can Can" was another song from a couple of years prior that I'd pay attention to when it played on the radio after becoming a minor R&B hit. But what stands out the most for me early on is their contribution to the day-in-the-life cult comedy, *Car Wash* which focused on a group of friends working at Sully Boyar's in a Los Angeles ghetto. The team meets a plethora of eccentric customers including a smooth-talking preacher played by Richard Pryor. In this short scene, he plays Daddy Rich, who arrives at the car wash in a gold Lincoln Continental stretch limousine with the Pointer Sisters in tow. The ladies burst into a secular song of worship, "You Gotta Believe," about the power of false belief.

At five years old, I didn't understand all of what I was watching in this film, which also included a moment of homophobic tension between young, militant car wash employee Duane/Abdullah, Bill Duke's debut film role, and flamboyant beauty-school student Lindy, played by Antonio Fargas. The scene had a friction I could recognize, even at that age. Antonio, perhaps best known as Huggy Bear from the 1970s TV show *Starsky and Hutch*, was so ahead of his time in portraying the cross-dressing, gender-bending character Lindy. Lindy quips with confident sensuality one of the film's most memorable lines, "I'm more man than you'll ever be and more woman than you'll ever get."

In 1978, the Pointer Sisters became a trio, with Bonnie Pointer leaving to go solo. They decided to do away with the 1940s nostalgic look and push their image and sound in a contemporary direction under the production of Richard Perry, who became their master hit-maker starting with a cover version of Bruce Springsteen's, "Fire." I was eight years old by this time, so I would continue to be a fan of the Pointer Sisters for the rest of their run.

They ushered in the '80s with soulful pop single, "He's So Shy" followed by a sultry number, "Slow Hand," about the joys of foreplay. Then came a string of hits that were made for this young teen who spent lots of time behind the closed doors of my childhood room, singing at the top of my lungs, "I'm So Excited," "Automatic," "Jump, For My Love" and "Neutron Dance," with the latter featured in the *Beverly Hills Cop* soundtrack. And MTV played their videos, one of the few acts of color in heavy rotation on the network. They received Grammy Awards for Best Pop Performance by a Duo or Group with Vocal for, "Jump, For My Love," and Best Vocal Arrangement for Two or More Voices for "Automatic."

Sadness hit the singing group in April 2006 when baby sister June died of lung cancer at the age of 52, surrounded by her sisters Anita and Ruth. The sisters have had an on-again, off-again relationship with Bonnie, who has also struggled with drug abuse while still maintaining a solo career. Since 2009, the group has consisted of Anita, Ruth, Ruth's daughter Issa and Ruth's granddaughter Sadako Pointer, with the members on rotation to ensure they have a trio whenever booked. In December 2016, *Billboard* ranked the Pointer Sisters as the 80th most successful dance artists of all time. The following year they were ranked as the fourth most popular girl group, ranking right under Destiny's Child, TLC and, of course, the Supremes.

Another sisters group consisted of Sister Sledge, who surely kept us dancing in the late '70s under the direction of Nile Rodgers and his Chic sound, including big hits like, "We Are Family" and "He's the Greatest Dancer." Soon-to-be Whitney's master producer, Narada Michael Walden was behind, "All American Girls" and Sledge also snagged a hit from Motown's catalog with Mary Wells', "My Guy." Their guest appearance on one of my favorite sitcoms, *The Jeffersons*, is among my favorites as well. Just weeks before the death of their sister Joni in March 2017, Sister Sledge buried a 30-year feud. The discord began between the sisters when sister Kathy released a solo album in 1989.

I remember being excited at the time at Kathy stepping out on her own as I adored her vocals on "We Are Family," especially the gospel-tinged ad-libs at the end of the song. Sister Sledge hadn't had a hit since 1985 with "Frankie." Because gossip didn't run as deeply then as it does now, during these social media times, I wasn't certain that there was a riff. But we'd find out years later there was.

The Jackson sisters are known to get along, perhaps because they don't work together. Although, at one time they did.

I loved seeing them all from 1976 to 1977 as stars of the first variety show where the entire cast was comprised of siblings. The thirty-minute Wednesday evening program began airing on CBS as a summer 1976 show and it continued into the 1976-1977 season, totaling twelve episodes by its wrap. Seeing the boys was old hat by this time, even for me, so watching the girls strut their stuff was a treat. They sang, danced and performed skits, most notable among them, Janet Jackson's Mae West impersonation that she'd bring with her to her next gig as Penny on *Good Times*. Joe Jackson did have the foresight to put Rebbie, La Toya and Janet together but the effort would be short-lived.

Instead, Latoya threw her hat in the ring as a solo artist, releasing a handful of minor hits, among them was 1980s "Night Time Lover," produced by her brother Michael, and 1984's "Heart Don't Lie," featuring Shalamar's Howard Hewitt and Musical Youth of "Pass the Dutchie" fame. The album of the same name is a favorite for other tracks such as "Bet'cha Gonna Need My Lovin'," "Hot Potato" and a cover of Prince's "Private Joy." *Full Force*, of Lisa Lisa & Cult Jam fame, produced a hip-hop number for Latoya in the late '80s. "You're Gonna Get Rocked" is what LaToya promised on that one.

Janet's legendary stats speak for themselves. Amidst stints on the TV series *Good Times*, *Different Strokes* and *Fame*. She debuted her solo music, with initial minor hits like "Young Love," "Say You Do" and "Don't Stand Another Chance." All valiant efforts, but the change in Janet's status from fan favorite to mega star was her Jimmy Jam & Terry Lewis debut collaboration, *Control*. And she stayed on that production ride to the sound of 100 million records sold, with the albums *Rhythm Nation 1814*, *Janet* and *The Velvet Rope* that feature some of the biggest hits of the '90s, including "Nasty," "When I Think of You," "Miss You Much," "Rhythm Nation," "Escapade," "Love Will Never Do," "That's The Way Love Goes" and "Together Again."

And don't forget oldest Jackson sister, Rebbie, of "Centipede" fame. Proof that Jackson support doesn't have to be on a stage or in the studio. I loved being in attendance when Rebbie escorted Janet to the New York premiere of the latter's Tyler Perry sequel, *Why Did I Get Married Too?* Rebbie's son Austin Brown, a singer, later accompanied Aunt Janet to the New York Premiere of *Tyler Perry's For Colored Girls*.

Superstar brother, Michael, has produced and/or recorded with all of them, with Latoya and Janet contributing to his jubilant smash "PYT (Pretty Young Thing)." His and Janet's "Scream" was everything, an inspired performance that came about as her growing popularity helped her struggling brother out. Michael's last twenty years of woes around allegations and lawsuits were in full swing by this time, though he continued to perform.

I happen to know personally two famous sisters who are like sisters to me. They are twins Tasha and Sidra Smith. Tasha is known for her loud girl animation in Tyler Perry's *Why Did I Get Married?* and its sequel, along with *Couples Retreat*. She also did a full run on OWN-TV's *For Better or Worse* and plays opposite Taraji P. Henson as Cookie's sister in *Empire*. Tasha also has two directorial credits to her name, a short film *Boxed In* and a TV One original movie *The Falicia Blakely Story*.

My sister's friend Sidra, with whom I have a close bond, is a NAACP Image Award-winning producer for the documentary *Free Angela and All Political Prisoners*, which is currently being adapted into a drama that she's also producing. *Free Angela* was directed by Shola Lynch and executive produced by Jada Pinkett Smith who Sidra personally brought onto the project. The film explores the turbulent months in 1972 that activist Angela Davis spent on trial for murder, conspiracy and kidnapping. She was later acquitted of all charges. To know Sidra is to know that she doesn't let the grass grow under her feet. When I met her, she'd already had short stints in the early '90s with acting and, prior to that, modeling in Paris. She was 19 at that time, when showrooms would hire her. Eventually, she landed like the character Mahogany, in Italy. But the impressions that will define her career and shape her legacy center around the work she does behind the scenes. After she shifted her career to casting music videos for Dr. Dre in the early '90s, she progressed quickly and moved to assisting on feature films. From there, she created Sidra Smith Casting, focusing on ad campaigns and TV commercials. And via her Gate Pass Entertainment company, she is adapting her 1999 feature film, A *Luv Tale*, into a series for a streaming outlet. The project is a love story between two women and stars MC Lyte, Tichina Arnold and Gina Rivera.

Siblings and family. We don't always get along, but something wonderful can be created if we can figure out how to support each other. I believe I've done well by my nephew and many of my young cousins who have their own aspirations. Yet, I look to one of the most powerful and bankable dynasties, The Smiths, for inspiration on how to be involved but hands off on the nuances of how the next generation gets down. When it comes to famous couples, Jada Pinkett Smith and Will Smith have twenty years of blended family bliss under their belts. They still look great together and are affirming testifiers to the good, bad and ugly of keeping it all together. Jada did a lot of work to have Will's son Trey be as much a part of the family as his younger siblings who come from her and Will. Before the tabloids could pin the scenario otherwise, we were watching Jada, Will's first wife Sheree Zampino and the rest of the kids, all together for family holidays and sometimes on the red carpet.

I looked to that harmonious example in my own life. Though the dynamics were different, my family was met with how we could embrace another into our fold after my dad decided to get remarried in 1997, a couple of years after our mom died. As a family unit, we all were still feeling a bit broken at the time. And in my case, we weren't dealing with the dynamics of minors. But the friction could be so heated at times as we navigated how we could embrace Dad's wife Diana, an irony not lost on anyone in my circle. It hasn't been perfect, and we still are not as close as we would likely be if Mom was still here. But we are a family and we respect each other on that level. I owe a lot of how I worked through that conflict to Jada.

Like my nephew Herman who has paved his own path, Jaden and Willow Smith are fierce, fearless and unafraid to express themselves through film, song, fashion and tweets. Willow has made hit records while Jaden has starred with his father in the Oscar nominated *The Pursuit of Happyness* and has since starred in the box office reboot *Karate Kid* as well as the Netflix series, *The Get Down*. They are shaping their own paths and utilizing what's been given to them with respect and allegiance.

Other kids didn't have it so good. The actress and comedian Rain Pryor has written about both the happy and difficult times in her relationship with her father in the book, *Jokes My Father Never Taught Me: Life, Love, and Loss With Richard Pryor*. She attributes aspects of her troubling childhood to her father's drug addiction more so than his profession. She stresses that he was very supportive of her in her career. At times, when she got a big head, Rain says her dad would be quick to get her in line. But as a father, sometimes paying hookers was more a priority than purchasing food. The extremes of celebrity life can be mind-blowing. Taking private jets and lavish vacations one day and Relying on food stamps and unemployment the next.

One of the most fascinating phenomena of Hollywood is the famous mother/daughters. It is complicated, enriching and unique, even without fame.

The uncanny resemblance that model and actress Zoe Kravitz has to her mother, actress Lisa Bonet, (her father is the rock star Lenny Kravitz) is uncanny. It is impossible to anyone familiar with Lisa's work on *The Cosby Show* and *A Different World* or her various film roles to watch Zoe perform and not immediately call to mind her mother.

Sometimes we get to watch mothers and daughters grow from turbulent times to being best friends. Other times, no matter how often the child has rebelled, their greatest influence on shaping who they are still can stem from a mom, whether she was present or not. With that, I wonder what it's like when the mother is a larger than life figure to the world! When she's everywhere including on television, billboards, the big screen and beyond.

How does the child appraise what is hopefully a pure version of love that lives underneath the sheen and shine required when a parent is famous, and the world adores them? Condola Rashad grew up watching her mother at work and knew from a very early age the commitment that a life in acting demanded. Phylicia took Condola with her on her jobs. "My mother took me everywhere when I was little." Condola said to industry bible *Backstage* in April 2017. "I got to witness the red carpets, the glitz and the glam and the shows." Condola knew the lifestyle to be fun but also hard work, and she got to see the process of going from rehearsal to opening night.

When Tracee Ellis Ross received a Golden Globe nod, famous mom Diana Ross took out a full-page ad in *The Hollywood Reporter* congratulating the *Black-ish* star on her Best Actress nomination. Tracee won, making her the second Ross in this lifetime to receive a Golden Globe. Diana won a Golden Globe in 1973 for Best New Actress for *Lady Sings the Blues*.

Ross has said she raised her kids when they were young but as adults, she just supports them and provides unconditional love. Rhonda has revealed that they weren't raised by nannies but by Miss Ross, which shows up so tangibly when you observe how they all just light up when they're around her. She didn't work on Christmas, New Year's or the kids' birthdays.

And to see the Ross clan is to know they support each other. They all come out when Miss Ross receives honors like the Presidential Medal of Freedom and the Kennedy Center Honor. If eldest boy Ross Arne Naess is getting married or opening his Los Angeles restaurant, Warwick, all in town are there. Chudney opened Books & Cookies in which Diana invested and all the Rosses patronize. In July 2017, Evan hosted a fabulous art gallery exhibit opening, showcasing his high-end pop paintings of icons that include his mom.

The oldest of her Ross' five children, Rhonda is also an Emmy-nominated actress from her impressive late-90s turn in the soap, *Another World*. An entrepreneur in her own right, Rhonda has also launched a real estate firm, but it's her singing that sustains her.

Backed by an eight-piece band, she performs her own songs, an amalgam of R&B, funk and jazz she calls "music of the African Diaspora." She and her mom toured thirty cities in summer 2017, with one of their stops being the main stage at the iconic Essence Music Festival. "When you're looking at me, I'm also looking at you," Miss Ross says in most of her shows to the audience right after she asks her lighting guy to turn the house lights up. I'm reminded that, as I have admired so many of these women for their talents and their entertainment, I also pay close attention to their lives. As I work through real life, they often provide cautionary tales and inspiration for how I can be the best son, brother, uncle and cousin. Famous or not, we're all truly more alike than we are different.

SCRAPBOOK

Rain Pryor and I were both recurring on-camera talent at Arise News Network in New York City. A freelance dispatch to interview her for "Oprah, Where Are They Now?" would have us meet up backstage at the Museum of Jewish Heritage in Battery Park City, NY for her one-woman show, "Fried Chicken and Latkes," which takes on her legendary dad Richard Pryor and other autobiographical topics. In her show, and to me, she speaks of how Diana Ross was the only one of her dad's friends who came to the funeral. She heard from few of them. Rain has come a long way since her breakout role on ABC sitcom, "Head of the Class."

Diana Ross' daughter, Rhonda Ross and I are buddies. I'm always at her jazz venues where she performs a range of jazz and neo-soul songs that she writes. For the last few years she's opened for her mom's summer concerts, including the main stage at Essence Music Festival. I also admire Tracee Ellis Ross. The Brown University graduate, is quick-witted and observant. She's won a Golden Globe for her hit sitcom, Blackish and has been nominated for an Emmy twice. She and her mom carry the distinction as the only mother-daughter combo to have hosted the American Music Awards, 31 years apart.

I've hosted Drums Along the Hudson in New York City for the last ten years. I was happy that Rhonda Ross was honored with the Humanitarian Award last June 2017.

Tracee and I snapped this on her August 2011 promo tour for the short-lived TV show, **Reed Between the Lines** in which she starred opposite Malcolm Jamal Warner.

Jillian Hervey is Vanessa Williams' second oldest daughter who is now known as Lion Babe. She's next level of Erykah Badu and all things Afro-pop!

I made sure to tell Jurnee Smollett how I enjoyed her performance in **The Great Debaters**. We were at the New York City premiere at the Ziegfeld Theatre December 2011.

Jurnee Smollett and her WGN **Underground** cast-mates attended the National Association of Black Journalists Convention in Minneapolis in August 2015. She's come a long way since "Eve's Bayou" in the '90s.

Before **Braxton Family Values** became the WE cable network smash hit, Tamar Braxton and her other sisters hoped to be a successful group. La Face Records wanted Toni Braxton. The other sisters signed with the music company Arista Records in 1989. One of the singles was a cover of Diana Ross' "The Boss." Soon after, Tamar went solo. In 1996, she made her debut with "So Many Ways." Then came an album and Tamar wouldn't record another album for 13 years. The second music album **Love and War** was a hit for Epic Records.

She chose Escualita, a gay bar near Manhattan's Port Authority as the backdrop for a **Love & War** CD release party. Her LGBTQ fans loved it.

My dear girlfriend Sidra Smith and I before I sang on the Gospel Uptown stage to Ashford & Simpson. I'm so blessed to have been able to share with them how much their talent and repertoire have meant to me. And I loved that my loved ones, like Sid, were there to support.

130 | THAT'S WHAT FRIENDS ARE FOR

Here I am sandwiched between two members of two of my favorite girl groups: Kathy Sledge, lead singer on Sister Sledge anthem "We Are Family" and Ruth Pointer, lead singer on Pointer Sisters hit from Eddie Murphy's blockbuster comedy Beverly Hills Cop, "Neutron Dance". We're backstage at the Historic Apollo Theater for a Bold Soul Sisters panel that took place February 2016.

Known for most of her life as Michael and Janet's really cute sister, Latoya is talented in her own right. In September 2013, I saw her in the starring role in **Tom D'Angora presents Newsical: The Musical**. She was absolutely wonderful and charming in her varied segments, including an impressive and satirical spin on Diana Ross. My friend , Karu Daniels, and I congratulated her backstage.

I stopped by 230 Fifth to toast LaToya Jackson on her book, **Starting Over** on July 2011

chapter 8

Talk Show Hosts

When *The Oprah Winfrey Show* launched in 1986, I was still in high school. After Oprah Winfrey overtook the venerable Phil Donahue as the top talk show host less than a year later, I no longer wanted to be a music legend, even declaring to the WTOC Savannah crew who covered my 1988 high school graduation speech that I hoped "to one day be the first black male Oprah Winfrey or to be working with her." During my senior year in high school, I ran the teleprompter for the school's 5 p.m. and 6 p.m. newscasts and determined that my career would be in the news business.

Just in time for my tenth high school reunion, I began working for *The Oprah Winfrey Show* as a senior field producer in fall 1998, scouting offsite locations, interviewing subjects remotely, and overseeing gathered footage. During my time on this job—which included interviewing President Bill Clinton from the White House's Roosevelt Room and Senator Barack Obama from Winfrey's home, meeting with 9/11 survivors and families of victims, and traveling to New Orleans in the wake of the devastation of Hurricane Katrina—I learned so much about the human condition from spiritual segments, human-interest stories, and my favorite beat: entertainment and celebrities.

One of my favorite episodes of Oprah Winfrey's show is when she revisited the life of Diana Ross, interviewing the singer's family and Billy Dee Williams, whose on screen relationship with Ross became the first iconic black romance. Because the production team knew I was a huge fan, they let me lead Ross from the green room backstage, through the sea of fans, and to the in-studio stage.

In another episode of Oprah Winfrey's show, she interviewed her former competitors: Sally Jessy Raphael, Geraldo Rivera, Ricki Lake, and Montel Williams, all of whom she had eclipsed by the time they retired their talk shows. When Winfrey retired her own show, I wasn't sure I could enjoy working with any other talent. She was the perfect teammate, always bringing her best self to work and expecting the same from everyone else. *The Oprah Winfrey Show* was a well-oiled machine, and I have yet to find a work environment just as supportive or deeply resourced.

Along the show's journey, Oprah Winfrey became much more than a wealthy celebrity talk show host. Now only did Winfrey use her star power to help elect America's first black president, but she also mentored a number of experts who now have their own talk shows: Dr. Phil, Dr. Oz, Suze Orman, Rachael Ray, and Iyanla Vanzant, to name just a few. And she inspired generations of black women to enter the talk business, including Tyra Banks, Whoopi Goldberg, Mo'Nique, and Wendy Williams.

In 2011, I became a senior field producer for *The Wendy Williams Show*, a nationally syndicated talk show since 2008. I work with Wendy Williams when she's on location for special packages and integrated marketing fare, and it's been a joy. She once called her glam squad, my partner, Ant, and me "the black gay elite of New York City." Williams is a fast worker and very present when you need her. She's also as professional as she is funny, and you can count on lots of laughs during shoots with her. And her show has been nominated for an Emmy twice. On her fiftieth birthday, the city council of Asbury Park, New Jersey, changed the name of the street where she grew up to Wendy Williams Way.

Before her television debut, Wendy Williams' fame came from her twenty years in the radio business. She became the self-proclaimed "Queen of All Media" during her New York heyday in the '90s, when she called people out on anything and everything. Perhaps her most famous moment was her infamous 2003 interview with Whitney Houston. A couple of weeks after Houston told ABC News *Primetime* host Diane Sawyer that "crack is whack," which became a common saying, Williams grilled the diva with questions about her drug and spending habits. Houston would have none of it, and her profanity-laced responses to Williams went viral. In 2009, Williams was inducted into the National Radio Hall of Fame.

In addition to Oprah Winfrey and Wendy Williams, I've worked with Nancy Grace, Geraldo Rivera, Al Roker, Dr. Oz, Rachael Ray, Kellie Pickler, Steve Harvey, Sherri Shepherd, and others. After a host of unique experiences with these personalities, I've found that not every talent is as easy to work with as Winfrey or Williams. Some require hand-holding, while others are so comical and friendly that you have to keep them on task. But as different as they all are, they do have one thing in common: even though they're incredibly wealthy and famous, they understand their audiences, always maintaining their relatability and empathy. Life would be so much better if it were more like a talk show: we would establish the dynamics, make sure all sides are represented, keep everything well-timed and flowing, and wrap it up with a smile, a prize, and a takeaway.

SCRAPBOOK

In April 2017, I attended the Washington, D.C., premiere of HBO's **The Immortal Life of Henrietta Lacks**, starring my old boss, Oprah Winfrey. I hadn't seen Winfrey in years, so I was glad to have a few minutes to catch up with her and snap this selfie with my nephew Herman and childhood BFF Ernest, as well as a handful of my nephew's friends.

Here Carla Hall and I are shown at her Southern Kitchen. **The Chew** co-host's counter-serve stand featuring Nashville-style chicken side dishes hadn't yet opened. From model to chef to TV personality, Hall's fame continues to grow. In 2016, she was selected to be the culinary ambassador for the National Museum of African American History and Culture's 400-seat Sweet Home Cafe.

I normally see Julie Chen on the CBS shows **Big Brother** and **The Talk**, but I got to talk to Chen and her husband, CBS head Les Moonves, following the opening night of **Motown: The Musical** in April 2013.

A member of Disney's Cheetah Girls, Adrienne Bailon Houghton became a co-host on **The Real**. Here she's shown posing on the runway before the February 2015 Michael Costello fashion show began.

Sunny Hostin was a prosecutor before she became a co-host on **The View**. Hostin also returned to ABC News as a senior legal correspondent and analyst in February 2016. As a host and legal analyst at CNN, she covered many high-profile trials, from George Zimmerman to Casey Anthony, and a number of other major stories, including the AME church shooting in Charleston and the confirmation of Eric Holder as U.S. attorney general.

TALK SHOW HOSTS | 141

After Sunny Hostin hosted the opening ceremony for the August 2016 joint convention of the National Association of Black Journalists and the National Association of Hispanic Journalists, I congratulated her on her new job as a full-time co-host on **The View**.

In August 2017, Sunny Hostin and I, along with our dear industry friend, **Good Morning America** correspondent Mara Schiavocampo, gathered with other ABC News journalists in New Orleans for a lovely meal. We were all scheduled to participate in industry panels the following day for a media gathering.

In October 2017, Sunny Hostin arranged for some friends and me to be in the audience on **The View**. It was exciting to see Whoopi Goldberg and the other ladies up close. I'm always amazed by how on-point yet kind and gracious Hostin is.

In August 2014, my journalist friend Karu Daniels invited me to go with him to see one of his clients, Wendy Williams, in **Chicago** on Broadway. It was one of her last performances that summer before she returned to her day job as a talk show host.

When Wendy Williams became a cover girl for **Essence** magazine in 2013, she invited me to the celebration. I'd just produced her show on location in the British Virgin Islands.

chapter 9
Television and Movie Star

It's doubtful any group in Hollywood struggles as much as black women to get quality work, and when they do, they are likely typecast. They don't get the covers of major fashion magazines or the lucrative perfume and jewelry endorsement deals that white B-list actresses easily come by. Even when a black male lead is cast, it's never a certainty that the significant other will be a black woman.

And nobody is defending them and celebrating them more than me and their many fans of the LGBTQ kind, primarily the little black boys who, like me, connected not only to the struggle of these actresses to work in a Hollywood that wasn't always casting in color. But once these women were cast, they played the parts, so we wouldn't forget them.

Never before have there been so many black actresses commandeering prime time television and box office success. Today, you can expect to find black actresses in any role, but these gains have been hard fought and slow coming.

Certainly, Hollywood's actresses know a thing or many about rejection. Black actresses have an especially difficult task because they are often playing the unseen and unheard, people who don't exist for many. They are playing historical figures whose narratives deserve more nuance to have us understand who these figures were. They are showing the humanity of women who are still imperfect but prove to be resilient through their struggles.

Their ability to pretend to be extraordinary makes them so. There is a range to how they approach the craft. Some were formally trained as thespians through college and workshops. while others come in with life experiences and the knowledge of many different kinds of people and situations. They understand the human condition and their curiosity is boundless. They do all of this while harboring great uncertainty about the future of their careers. They may go unemployed for months and even sometimes years.

My admiration for these women extends to soap operas as well. It's worth noting that my mother raised both of her boys to love the CBS soaps. We had to tell her what was happening and to whom, ifwhom if the VCR didn't catch a particular episode. For years we've watched *The Young and the Restless* and *The Bold and the Beautiful*. Before they were canceled, *As the World Turns* and *Guiding Light* were also in our rotation. My brother and I are not the closest of friends, but we do generally get along. One distinct pastime that connects us is the stories. We may not speak for weeks, but if Victor Newman from *Y&R* does something crazy, we are on that phone talking about it as if these folks are real. When our favorite actresses from these shows hit new highs, we get excited. Nia Long started on *Guiding Light* before becoming a renowned film actress. For years, Tamara Tunie played attorney Jessica on, *As The World Turns*. And Anna Maria Horsford, aka Thelma from *Amen*, later joined the cast of *B&B*.

Through it all, black actresses have to maintain optimism and a great deal of stamina! Physical stamina, yes, but also stamina of the heart and mind because there will be rejections. They must banish self-doubt after the 100th rejection. There is sexism, ageism and colorism, which plays to the light-skinned/dark-skinned wars we've seen people of color place on each other. Spike Lee underscored that dynamic in black culture in his movie, *School Daze*. Actresses like his sister, Joie Lee, were Jigaboos, a label given to darker hued college students. They had an arch rivalry with the Wannabees, who were light or mixed and often the objects of certain black men's desires. Coming from the south, I also know how much people can have color complexes, proclaiming pride over having some Native American in them. "My grandmother's Cherokee," some say as a badge of honor for having lighter skin. And that game of shade transcends into the pores of Hollywood and its castings. So, while being optimistic, brown actresses must manage expectations.

Contrary to the behind-the-scenes sheen of my primary profession as a TV producer, I have put myself out there for featured talent work and have landed several spot host gigs. In 2003, I booked TLC's *The Good, the Bad, & the Ugly* and ESPN-2's, *Cold Pizza*. Two high profile opportunities to be seen and produced by someone else. Though I didn't have a talent agent at the time, I was attracting lots of auditions, some of which turned into work. Later that year, I was submitted for *Queer Eye for the Straight Guy*, having attracted a talent agent from ICM. She committed to work with me on a project-by-project basis. Producers Collins and Metzler ran a round-robin of exhausting combo tests between hundreds and hundreds of gay men. I was going out for the culture guy, who was eventually Jay Rodriguez. The other four fabs around whom Jay worked with were the four with whom I auditioned. In fact, Collins and Metzler had me lunch at B. Smith to tell me they were presenting me with those four to Bravo. In the end, the network chose otherwise. I found out from my agent that they loved me but thought I might be too "strong" a personality opposite Carson Kressley, though we got along splendidly.

NBC purchased Bravo and ordered twelve episodes of the series. NBC promoted the show extensively, including billboard campaigns and print advertisements in national magazines. I was crushed but clear that disappointment comes with any high-stakes pursuit. You win some and you lose some.

Out of that opportunity, my agent arranged my getting an invitation to audition for a pilot, a gay version of *The View* by the *Hard Copy* producers. This was back when the success of *Queer Eye* made producers feel that all things gay were good. If the enterprise had succeeded, it would have been a daytime talk show with six men offering a gay take on entertainment, fashion, lifestyle and the daily news. In

View terms, they considered me their Meredith Viera, the moderator for the show.

The pilot taping took place at CBS Studios and went very well. We were retained by the production company to not go out for anything else while they tried to sell the show. We had a couple of close call suitors. But in the end, the pilot wasn't picked up. The production company instead green-lighted, *Life & Style*, a panel show with Kimora Lee Simmons that didn't last past its first season.

These experiences have strengthened who I am as a professional because I am so clear that I have to continue to put my best impression forth, whether I get the gig or not. At one point, I may have told myself I was too effeminate to be a male on-camera talent. One of my college TV professors told me as much. "Watch that effect," she said, gesturing her hands in a wand of fabulous flourish. And she said it like a concerned mother, albeit a homophobic one. "You won't be able to be on camera like that." That wasn't true as I was a reporter trainee right out of college and got the chance to sharpen my entertainment interviewing skills on-camera, starting in 1992.

A few years after that, my main and most lucrative client, *The Oprah Winfrey Show*, would sometimes ask me to break the fourth wall as a producer and be on camera with that very flourish I was told wouldn't play in Peoria. Sometimes, I was in Peoria for those shoots. From being myself, I got the chance to see the industry welcome, "my kind." With that has come opportunity. I have booked some cool projects over the years, but I haven't landed yet a sustaining, dream gig as a TV talent.

Still, I've continued to be a respected player in this industry as a producer and as a talent. And without having attracted certain representation that might have been able to make this industry ride go more effortlessly, I've been steering a lot of my career to a very successful effect in the grand scheme of my life's timeline.

Understanding that and navigating a still impressive career inside of social and industry realities is exactly what I see African American actresses address within the game of Hollywood, which hasn't always been, as Langston Hughes noted in a famed poem, "a crystal stair."

One of my favorite times of year is awards season, in large part because when one of these ladies' wins, they are testifying to their triumphs over oppression and rejection. In their daily life, few people would give them the time to communicate the struggle. For those who win, it's a time when they get to say it. Halle Berry said it through tears when she was the first African-American woman to win a Best Actress Oscar for her role in *Monster's Ball*. Across platforms, we have seen Viola Davis make us cry in her human telling of hunger, poverty, struggle and accomplishment. Viola Davis, nominated for three Academy Awards, is the only black actress to win the Triple Crown of Acting, winning an Oscar, Emmy and Tony. I remember crying along with Vanessa Williams in 1989 during the NAACP Image Awards as I'd inherited an investment in seeing her return to popularity and grace after being stripped of her Miss America crown after some salacious pictures were published of her in the nude. Like a friend, I just wanted success for her. Through her acceptance speech, I knew I wasn't alone as someone who was rooting for her. "I definitely want to thank the black community," Vanessa said. "When I needed you, you were there for me. I thank you for giving me the opportunity and encouragement. For showing me how to spread my wings and fly because I'm flying now. Thank you!"

I know the message landed. In more recent years, a decade into the 2000s, it has been an especially festive time as black actresses have been recognized much more than in the past, though still not as much as they should be.

And one of the most interesting phenomena has been seeing movie stars make their way to the small screen for juicy roles. Halle Berry may have been the first African-American actress to win a Best Actress Oscar for her role in Monsters Ball but she also translated her success into TV accomplishments including a Best Actress Emmy, Golden Globe and NAACP Image Award for her portrayal of the first African-American woman to receive a Best Actress nomination from the Academy Awards, Dorothy Dandridge. She'd later go on to executive produce and star in her 2015 CBS show, *Extant*.

Whoopi Goldberg, who was first nominated for an Oscar as a lead actress in *The Color Purple*, won for her supporting role in *Ghost*, but has brought her EGOT status to the moderator post on *The View* for over a decade. It's quite inspiring as the caravan of stars come to the talk show to promote their projects, and often these A-list guests are simply excited to be in Whoopi's midst, given she's won Emmy, Grammy, Oscar and Tony awards. Between Taraji P. Henson and Kerry Washington, multiple Academy and Emmy nominations have been earned, but we've watched TV transform them into household names for an even wider audience than their film jobs have offered. *Scandal* creator Shonda Rhimes booked Kerry Washington to play Olivia Pope in the political thriller for which she was nominated many times through the show's seven season run, ushering in space for the likes of Taraji P. Henson's Cookie Lyons on the Fox hit *Empire*, playing opposite Terrence Howard who is the fictional music mogul Lucious Lyons. Soon Viola Davis would juggle her award-winning film work in fare like *The Help* and *Fences* with a major TV lead role from Shondaland, *How To Get Away With Murder?,Murder?* for which she received an Emmy in 2015.

Mo'Nique is someone I came to adore via TV as she was Nicky Parker, mother of Kim Parker, who was featured on *Moesha*, opposite Brandy before a hit spinoff. From 1999 to 2004, I got so many belly laughs watching the shenanigans of *The Parkers*. Whenever it pops up in syndication, I will still be a captive audience. But as a twist of fate goes, Mo'Nique in 2010 became an Academy Award winning Best Supporting Actress for her riveting performance as the abusive mother to Gabourey Sidibe in Lee Daniels' *Precious*.

Octavia Spencer and Viola Davis both expressed concerns to me about what people would say of them accepting a 2011 role in *The Help* in which they each played Jackson, Mississippi-based maids during the Civil Rights Movement in 1962. The plot focuses on a young white woman, aspiring journalist Eugenia "Skeeter" Phelan, played by Emma Stone. She interviews a number of black maids on their treatment by their white bosses, including Aibileen Clark and Minny Jackson, played by Viola and Octavia. Octavia won the Best Supporting Actress Oscar in 2012.

There was less criticism about Lupita Nyong'o's portrayal of an enslaved woman in *12 Years a Slave*. The film received acclaim all around and earned almost $190 million worldwide on a $22 million production budget. And Lupita's Best Supporting Actress Oscar continued the tradition of black women making a splash.

Playing in excellence despite the type of role or the size of the screen is how these women often navigate their careers, so we can see them still standing. And many of them have been able to share that, whenthat when they've won awards or in interviews they give to the press. As they share the story of how they weren't seen for certain parts or how they were afraid to do this kind of a part for what the black community might say, I can put myself in their shows and film work in my own career.

And many of them have been able to share that when they've won awards or in interviews they give to the press.

SCRAPBOOK

Cicely Tyson is a living icon known for modeling, acting and unwavering support for civil rights. Throughout her career, I strongly believe that she has served as an inspiration and active participant in the movement to expand the role of women in the entertainment industry. At the age of 91, Cicely Tyson was given America's highest civilian honor; The Presidential Medal of Freedom at the White House by Barack Obama who was the first African-American president. Among her notable works are **Sounder, The Autobiography of Miss Jane Pittman,** and **The Help**. I have interviewed her a number of times together with other acting legends. But each time I talk to her I am still left in awe with her eloquence and animation. Her dynamic character is mirrored in her dramatic storytelling and use of pauses for a stunning effect.

Cicely Tyson, Lenny Kravitz and my friend Colman Domingo at the premiere of Lee Daniel's **The Butler** in June 2013. I was escorting Colman that night as a favor to his publicist and our common friend. Lauren Tobin of Panther Biz Media.

TELEVISION AND MOVIE STAR | 155

Judy Pace, sex goddess of early Blaxploitation films, went on to play in the TV shows, **Peyton Place** and **The Young Lawyers**. I chatted with Pace and her daughter Julie Pace Hightower of the soap opera, **The Young & the Restless** in San Diego in Summer 2010.

I bumped into Kellita Smith, best known for her role as Wanda McCullough in the Fox sitcom **The Bernie Mac Show**, during New York's Fashion Week in September 2010.

Since her breakout role as Terri Joseph from the TV adaptation of the feature film **Soul Food**, Nicole Ari Parker has had a wonderful career. Her husband and frequent co-star, Boris ,was a cousin of my first love, Kodjoe and his funeral was where I first met the actress. We've seen each other several times since including during her Broadway run of A Streetcar Named Desire. These photos were taken in Spring 2012 as I got to reacquaint myself with Nicole Ari Parker as she prepared to co-star in the multicultural.

I met Vanessa Bell Calloway at Oz and Lynne Scott's Sherman Oaks estate. At the invitation of publicist, Lauren Tobin, was attending the Jackie Robinson Foundation's annual Jazz on the Green. Vanessa, with nearly a dozen NAACP Image Award nominations, had a small but memorable role of Princess Imani Izzi in Eddie Murphy's comedy, **Coming to America**. Since then she's had roles in movies including **What's Love Got to Do with It**, and most recently, **Southside with You** and has also been a popular character on the TV show, **Shameless**.

At the Paris Theatre in New York City for the premiere of **Belle** starring British actress, Gina Prince-Blythewood and director Amma Asante on April 28, 2014.

I ran into Yvette Nicole Brown at **Essence Magazine's** cover party for Wendy Williams. She came with her dear friend Sherri Shepherd who I would produce the next week at the NYC Auto Show for **The View**. It was nice to meet Sherri before we started working together. We had a blast on our shoot.

When she was nominated for an Oscar for "Precious," many thought it was a fluke. However, Gabourey Sidibe continues to be booked, including her current role as Becky on Fox hit **Empire**.

Gabourey Sidibe was nominated for an Oscar for her gut-wrenching role in the Lee Daniels film Executive Produced by Oprah Winfrey and Tyler Perry.

Actress and author Tanya Wright stopped by Arise Entertainment 360 to talk about her work with "The Oliver Scholarship," a mentoring and scholarship program for New York City youth. Tanya played one of Malcolm Jamal Warner's girlfriends on **The Cosby Show**.

Danielle Brooks is best known for her role as Tasha "Taystee" Jefferson on the Netflix original series, **Orange Is the New Black**, and for her Tony-nominated portrayal of Sofia in the 2015 Broadway production of **The Color Purple**.

Danielle Brooks is an Affirming sister. She attended the Out 100 in December 2015 and was such a joy with whom to party with! She's got a nice, southern way.

The world loves Anna Maria Horsford from her iconic portrayal of Deacon Frye's daughter, Thelma, on the 1980s hit NBC sitcom **Amen**. She continues to work currently as a Daytime Emmy nominee on CBS soap **The Bold & The Beautiful**. She plays the mother of a transgender woman.

I'd met Anna Marie Horsford a time or few. But May 2013 at the 3rd anniversary of Harlem Cove, she and I hit it off. The soap opera lover that I am, I immediately began to chat about her role on her CBS soap.

In 1991, Lynn Whitfield won the Emmy Award for her portrayal of Josephine Baker in an HBO film, but her career spans 30 years. She's a twice married mother of an adult daughter, she's attracted a new burst of popularity and next-level artistry in her portrayal of mega-church first lady, Lady Mae, on the Oprah Winfrey Network's **Greenleaf**.

TELEVISION AND MOVIE STAR | 161

Lynn Whitfield called me over to pose with her on the step at Thurgood Marshall College Fund's 24th Anniversary Dinner at the Metropolitan Ballroom on October 24, 2011 in New York.

Lynn Whitfield and her mom with me at the 65th Anniversary of the Links Incorporated in Washington DC.

American singer and actress known for her Tony Award-winning performance in the Broadway production of **Caroline or Change** and her starring role as Lorrell Robinson in the 2006 film **Dreamgirls**. She also starred as Tiana, an African American princess in Walt Disney Pictures' 2009 animated film **The Princess and the Frog**. In 2014, Rose played the role of Beneatha Younger in the Broadway revival of **A Raisin in the Sun**, for which she was nominated for the Spring 2013 at the Belle NYC Premier at the Paris Theatre in New York.

At the For Colored Girls art exhibit with Tessa Thompson in February 2011 and at a press meet & greet in January 2009 as the cast of **Cat on a Hot Tin Roof** prepared to do their first rehearsal under the direction of Debbie Allen.

Tichina during the intermission of FELA in Los Angeles January 2012. We just stumbled into each other.

Spring 2014 brought Tichina to Harlem.

Drums Along the Hudson honored Tichina Arnold as a humanitarian June 2015.

I got the chance to reconnect with my Morehouse brother Rockmond Dunbar who played opposite Vanessa Williams in the TV show **Soul Food**. We were all gathered in Philadelphia for a screening of a film they also shot together, "Raising Izzie."

We all remember Kimberly Elise in **Set It Off** with Queen Latifah, Vivica A. Fox and Jada Pinkett Smith. That was her debut, but she's gone on to do much critically acclaimed work including **Beloved, John Q, The Manchurian Candidate, Diary of a Mad Black Woman, The Great Debaters,** and **For Colored Girls**. Her most recent role was a departure: VH1 comedy-drama series, **Hit the Floor**. She has won four NAACP Image Awards.

Here at Tim Palen's Living Portraits opening night reception at NYC's Lehmann Maupin Gallery in October 2010. The exhibition featured moving still-images of the cast of Tyler Perry's adaptation of the choreo-poem by Ntozake Shange, **For Colored Girls**.

Malinda Williams and I in November 2010 at an industry event that was held at Ogilvy. She is best known for her portrayal of Bird in the Showtime series **Soul Food**.

May 2011, congratulating Sanaa Lathan on her Off-Broadway performance as Vera Stark, an African-American maid featured in critically acclaimed Lynn Nottage play.

At a press event to promote BET's **Reed Between the Lines**, Melissa DeSouza who played Tracee Ellis Ross' sidekick on the show was in attendance.

Daphne Maxwell Reid is best known for her role as the second Vivian Banks on the NBC sitcom **The Fresh Prince of Bel-Air** from 1993 until 1996.

November 2011, I got the chance to produce the 65TH Anniversary video for Links Inc. which meant Ant and I got to attend the DC-based gala and meet hosts Daphne Maxwell Reid and her husband Tim Reid.

Cassie dated my friend Ike, one of my straight buddies in New York City. He wanted my approval of her, so we met on one of their dates and I approved. She was so warm and funny and had a Southern breeze to her. Turns out we had folks in common from where she grew up in Tallahassee, so our bond is rooted in instinct and actual history. When we have downtime, we have had the chance to hang out.

January 2012, we all attended the Red Tail World premiere with George Lucas in the house to support our friend Nate Parker who portrayed one of the Tuskegee Airmen. **(previous page)**

June 2016, my friend Theo and I attended the premiere of **The Real MVP**, a cable movie starring Cassie as the mother of NBA superstar, Kevin Durant.

Keesha Sharp attended the **Red Tails** premiere at the Ziegfeld Theater on January 10. I was excited to meet her as she portrayed one of my favorite characters, Monica, on the sitcom **Girlfriends**. She now has a role in the **Lethal Weapon** reboot as the wife of Damon Wayans.

I was a regular pop culture analyst on TV **One's Life After**, a weekly show that updates the viewing audience on pop culture icons. Screenwriter Tina Andrews known for writing the **Why Do Fools Fall In Love**? script about the life of Frankie Lymon from the Teenagers was a 70s actress who played opposite Jimmie Walker in **Good Times** and LeVar Burton in **Roots**. We both filmed our commentary at the same time in New York City on April 2013.

Regina Taylor is known for her 1993 Golden Globe Award-winning role as Lily Harper. It was a rare moment in that time in which the Best Actress in a Television Drama was African American. **I'll Fly Away** put her on the map, but she's continued to stay true to her artistry via TV projects like USA Network's **DIG** about which I got to interview her on an entertainment magazine show I was hosting in 2014. Currently, Regina, the playwright and director, is the Denzel Washington Endowed Chair in Theater for Fordham's theater program.

TELEVISION AND MOVIE STAR | 169

It was great to interview Zabryna Guevara on Arise Entertainment 360. She spoke about her role on Gotham and how it allows her to stretch in ways she never did in prior work like **The Sopranos** and **Law & Order**.

Vivica A. Fox is the great example of a hustle! And she's been doing it a long time! From Indiana to Hollywood, she started on soap operas and Patti Labelle's sitcom **Out All Night**. Then, roles in **Set It Off, Independence Day,** and **Booty Call** would cement her as one of Hollywood's most versatile actresses and she is always booked. I got to interview her along with the rest of her cast from **Chocolate City**.

Vivica at the Oscar consideration luncheon for the documentary Free Angela. Our friend Sidra Smith and the Free Angela team won the NAACP Image Award. My girlfriend Sidra was working on a project to star Vivica A. Fox on the development tip. I was cast to be one of the characters for a reading.

Interviewing Vivica A. Fox and the rest of her cast Robert Ri'chard and Darren Dewitt Henson on a guest hosting day at Arise Entertainment 360. I loved that Vivica gave us just as much energy as she did the A-list shows. She's a class act and a true diva in the best sense of the word. May 2015.

In addition to Sheryl Lee Ralph and Jennifer Holliday, Loretta Devine is an Original **Dreamgirl** from the Broadway musical, the only original to get placement in the feature film with Beyonce, Eddie Murphy and Jennifer Hudson. She moved from the Great White Way to Hollywood and has 40 years of great work to show for it including **Waiting To Exhale, The Preacher's Wife , For Colored Girls,** and **Jumping the Broom**. She may be best known for her roles as Marla Hendricks in **Boston Public** and **Grey's Anatomy** for which she won a Primetime Emmy Award for Outstanding Guest Actress in a Drama Series in 2011.

I got another opportunity to connect with Loretta Devine at the Judge Mablean Father's Day Brunch in 2009 and at the **For Colored Girls** premiere in Spring 2011.

I was first introduced to Jenifer Lewis as one of the Fresh Prince's aunts. Then, I discovered she'd done pre-Jennifer Holliday Effie in a workshop phase of **Dreamgirls**. Nell Carter was also in that mix before Holliday came along. And via roles in **What's Love Got To Do With It, Preacher's Wife** and even **Girlfriends** as Toni Childs' mom Rhetta, Jenifer became The Mother of Hollywood. Wrote a New York Times Best Seller about that very life's journey. Another TV film favorite, **Jacki's Back**, a mockumentary of an aging diva trying to make a stage comeback. It's a guilty pleasure for the LGBTQIA set. Meanwhile, she's the Mom on "Black-ish."

Orlando, June 2013. I coordinated Remy Martin as the spirits sponsor for this event while Jenifer Lewis was there to promote her film David E. Talbert's **Baggage Claim**.

12 years ago, Tika Sumpter was the host for a reality show called **Best Friend's Date**. Her first film project was the musical **Stomp the Yard: Homecoming in 2010**. She was also in **Salt** in the same year. After a series of films like **Ride Along** and **A Madea Christmas**, she took a part with the Oprah Winfrey Network. America loves to hate her character Candace Young.

I met Tika Sumpter at the BET Premiere of **The Game** at Butter in Downtown Manhattan. It was a January night that brought a blizzard by the end of the party. **Being Mary Jane** premiered in 2013, but I was invited to an early screening of it at the Urban World Film Festival here in New York City. Tika Sumpter was featured in the original movie before transitioning to Tyler Perry's **Have & The Have Nots**.

After graduating high school in Atlanta, Jasmine received a scholarship to attend the Alvin Ailey Dance Center in New York. Enter Whitley Gilbert and her iconic role as a Southern Belle on The Cosby Show spin-offSpin-off **A Different World**. She won the NAACP Image Award every year she was on the show. Her film credits include Spike Lee's **School Daze** and the film **Harlem Nights**. In addition to more TV and stage roles, she recorded a Top 40, self-titled R&B album in 1990 featuring dance hit "Try Me" and went on to have roles in numerous films, televisions shows and stage productions. She's currently featured in **The Quad** on BET back on a fictional campus like Hillman College, but as an administrator this time. In a small, school daze turn, Jasmine Guy's dad Rev. Dr. Guy taught me Religion at Morehouse.

Got the chance to greet Jasmine Guy June 2013 at Sundae Sermon at an outdoor house party. Told her I was a Morehouse Man as her father, Dr. William Guy, was our Religion & Philosophy professor.

I met Leslie Uggams at the Broadway Inspirational Voices Summer Concert at First Corinthian Baptist Church in May 2014.

I ran into Monique Coleman in May 2014 at the Broadway Inspirational Voices Summer Concert at First Corinthian Baptist Church. She remembered our moment when she helped me win $25,000 on Million Dollar Password.

I've loved Tamara Tunie since she was introduced as attorney. Jessica, on one of my CBS soaps **As The World Turns**. During most of her time on the daily story, Tamara was often on double duty with primetime efforts. She's been a cast member of **Law & Order Special Victims Unit** as Dr. Melinda Warner. She's had other primetime, procedural success with Fox's 24, the ABC cop series NYPD **Blue**.

Gina from **Martin**'s mom is played by Judy Ann Elder. Of course, she's done much more. The actress, director, writer also played the most recent Harriet Winslow on ABC's sitcom with Steve Urkel, **Family Matters**.

I met Judy in L.A. at the home of Hollywood director Oz Scott.

Quite the renaissance woman, Amanda Seales has become known of late as a co-star on HBO hit **Insecure** starring Issa Rae, though she's been hustling on all platforms and stages throughout her career. Her film work includes 1993 movie **Cop and a Half**. The next year Seales was featured on the Nickelodeon sitcom, **My Brother and Me**. Russell Simmons' Def Poetry Jam gave Amanda Diva a platform that extended to gigs on MTV2 and beyond. She also sings and considered a full-out recording career before deciding to focus on acting and stand-up comedy.

Amanda Diva's one woman show **Death of the Diva** did a fun run in February 2012 in New York City.

Black audiences first got to know Halle Berry for role on **Strictly Business** and Spike Lee's **Jungle Fever** in which she portrayed a crack-addicted woman. From BAPS to **Catwoman** to **Losing Isaiah** to **Gothika**, Halle has delivered a range of film work.

At her NYC Premiere of **Frankie & Alice** in November 2010, it was great to grab a moment with Halle Berry on her role as a paranoid schizophrenic.

TELEVISION AND MOVIE STAR | 177

In 2010, I got the chance to produce the script and evening for Mary J. Blige's FFAWN which Taraji P. Henson hosted. According to guest and social networking buddy Lynn Whitfield, "This event ran smoothly and was well-paced! GREAT JOB!" Her words. THANKS LYNN!

Lupita Amondi Nyong'o, who attended Yale's drama school and won the Best Actress Oscar for 12 Years A Slave, is just getting started. Her next big thing after the Academy Awards was playing a teenage orphan in the critically acclaimed 2015 play **Eclipsed** for which she received a Tony nomination.

August 2011. **The Help** stars Viola Davis and Oscar winner for her role in this film, Octavia Spencer came to watch their movie with 800 journalists at the National Association of Black Journalists (NABJ) Convention's special pre-release film screening and panel discussion.

February 2013. On contract with Remy Martin as a Brand Ambassador at the time, I partnered the fine liquor company with the African American Black Film Critics Association for its Oscar Viewing Party. Viola Davis received a special honor that night.

CBS soap **Guiding Light** was her first gig out of high school. Since she was booked and didn't choose to go to college, she was available to attract **Boyz n the Hood**. And her career continued to take off from there including being paired with Will Smith in television series **The Fresh Prince of Bel-Air. In Too Deep, Friday, Soul Food, and Love Jones** are among her other iconic film titles. When Chris Rock did the documentary **Good Hair**, Nia helped him promote it.

I moderated a screening of Chris Rock's **Good Hair** with he and Nia Long. I remember the mic that Chris and Nia were to share went out so we ALL had to share. Though Nia seemed none too pleased with the snafu, she played nice and was generous of spirit during our talk.

Tim Palen's Living Portraits opening night reception at NYC's Lehmann Maupin Gallery in October 2010. The exhibition featured moving still-images of the cast of **For Colored Girls**, Tyler Perry's latest drama, out November 5. Janet hosted the event and met up with her For Colored Girls co-stars Kerry Washington and Anika Noni Rose and photographer Tim Palen.

In 2018, Alfre Woodard may be known as Cookie's mom on Fox drama **Empire**. She's a new addition to the Spring 2018 season. But the Tulsa, Oklahoma native has had extensive success in Hollywood dating back to the '80s with **St. Elsewhere**, and pushing through to the more current Netflix series **Luke Cage**.

September 2011. Reacquainted with Alfre after Legends at the Premiere of Steel Magnolias. in New York City at the Aris Theatre.

Alabama native Octavia Spencer landed her first acting role while working behind the scenes of 1996's **A Time to Kill**. Small parts in shows like **City of Angels** and **The Chronicle** got her to 2011 when her career shot to the top as she earned an Academy Award for her role as a maid in **The Help**. Rolls in **Fruitvale Station, Get on Up, Black or White, Insurgent**, and **Allegiant** have kept her in the spotlight. Recent roles in 2017's **The Shape of Water** and 2016's biopic **Hidden Figures** have kept her Oscar nominated.

Octavia Spencer won an Oscar for her role in **The Help**. She and Viola Davis screened the movie before a packed house of black journalists in August 2011 before it went into wide release. Both actresses were nervous at how the audience would receive it. The film received a standing ovation.

Kim Coles and I are buddies so as our respective careers can keep us on the road, we are good to grab a bite and a hug as we did here at Vinyl in New York City. It was November 2011, so we did an early birthday toast.

Sherri Shepherd was, early on, known as the black girl on all the white sitcoms including **Suddenly Susan, Everybody Loves Raymond**, and more. Then, from continuing to do stand-up comedy, game show hosting, and additional acting roles, she came into America's household as a Barbara Walters-endorsed co-host, from 2007 to 2014, winning one Daytime Emmy during that time.

APRIL 2012. With Yvette Nicole Brown and Sherri Shepherd at ESSENCE Magazine cover party for Wendy Williams. Yvette and Sherri are girlfriends. I knew that from having watched **The View** earlier that day. I'd just wrapped up my 13 years with **The Oprah Winfrey** Show as it had just gone off the air, or was about to, and in my post-Oprah diversification, I attracted The View as a recurring freelance client.

She is the half-sister of Nia Long who played in **The First Friday**. She attended Morris Brown College in Atlanta, Georgia where movies like **Drumline** and **Stomp the Yard** were filmed.

Comedian Sommore at BET Networks New York Upfront. April 2013.

In 2010, Nash put on her dancing shoes to compete on **Dancing With the Stars**. She didn't win her season, but she added to her growing fan base. Two years later, Nash began starring in the TV comedy **The Soul Man** with Cedric the Entertainer. She also had a leading role in the HBO hospital sitcom **Getting On**. The role earned Nash her first Emmy nomination. In 2014, Nash made guest appearances on **The Mindy Project**. In 2015 she moved on to the horror comedy **Scream Queens** with Emma Roberts and Jamie Lee Curtis.

For Colored Girls Premiere Screening, The Ziegfeld Theatre. October 2010 **(left photo)** and at The Soul Man Media Mixer Crosby Hotel NYC. March 2014 **(right photo)**.

Chloe Hilliard is a larger than life comedian and I met her when she was 16 years old and learning about journalism in the New York Association of Black Journalism Workshop which in 2005, I Co-Directed. She was funny then and I wasn't surprised when after a successful post-college career in journalism that she would become a comedian. She made her national TV debut on NBC's smash hit **Last Comic Standing** and has additional credits on **Gotham Comedy Live**, Comedy Central's **The Nightly Show**, Tru TV's **Almost Genius** and MTV's **Acting Out**.

Child star Raven-Symoné who we adored on **The Cosby Show** and **Hangin' With Mr. Cooper** matured further to find success on Disney's **That's So Raven** and Broadway's 2013 adaptation of **Sister Act**. From there, she did a stint on **The View** as a co-host before returning to Disney for a reboot, **Raven's Home** in which she's the mother of two kids, one with special visions.

Here with Raven Symone in Puerto Rico at the Xscape Arts & Music LGBT event. So proud of Raven on her journey for truth and self-acceptance. Memorial Day 2016.

TELEVISION AND MOVIE STAR | 185

Our first moment was at the **For Colored Girls** Pre-Premiere art exhibit at which Anika Noni Rose introduced me to her co-star ,"Tessa? Do you know Life of Riley? Shall we get a picture?"

Our 2nd moment was when I interviewed her at a press conference for a Kenny Leon-directed play in which Tessa was starring. We bonded on the diversity concerns in Hollywood as "Oscars So White" was ripe at that time.

With Jurnee Smollett for **Great Debaters**. Ziegfeld Theater in New York for the PREMIERE.

Our 2nd moment was at NABJ in Minneapolis as she and the **Underground** cast came to promote their first season.

Tatyana Ali is best known as Ashley Banks who she played from 1990 to 1996 on the NBC hit **The Fresh Prince of Bel-Air**. She got the help from Will Smith who played her big cousin on the show when she was ready to start her singing career on the last season of the show. Her single, "Daydreamin" was certified gold within weeks of its release and it went to #6 and remained for a few weeks. In addition to more television and movies, she also went to Harvard and graduated with a degree in Anthropology in June 2002. In addition to more performing and recently becoming a wife and a mother, Tatyana also produces her own projects alongside her sister.

Wallis received a nomination for the Academy Award for Best Actress, and the first person born in the 21st century nominated for an acting Oscar. The prized role was Hushpuppy. The project was Beasts of the Southern Wild. Additionally, she starred in the Annie remake, for which she received a Golden Globe nomination for Best Actress in a Motion Picture, Comedy or Musical.
Ebony Power 100 Gala at Jazz at Lincoln. November 2012.

chapter 10

Reality Stars

As I stated in the previous chapter, I grew up watching soap operas with my mother. Yet one by one, I've been having to grieve as my favorite long-running soap operas were taken off the air. First, it was *Guiding Light* in 2009, then *As the World Turns* in 2010. Plus, there were a few shows on ABC and NBC that I missed when they were canceled, including *General Hospital* and *Another World*, though I wasn't watching them at the time of their demise.

Though I have been upset about the cancellations, I understand the industry analysis regarding its declining viewership, which resulted in sponsors backing out. Like anything that goes down, something in the marketplace that's new, exciting, perhaps cheaper to produce, is in its wake: reality TV. Pushed to the periphery of television for much of their history, black women of the reality TV genre commanded center stage. Before Shondaland took over ABC's lineup, which ushered in space for Kerry Washington, Viola Davis, Debbie Allen, Cicely Tyson and more to present a fuller, more layered set of African American images—imperfect and in better packaging, like what my reality looks like—a proliferation of franchises such as *Real Housewives, Love & Hip Hop, Basketball Wives, Baller Wives* and so forth (... I could go on and on) have shifted the paradigm. These shows received a fair amount of criticism for being disgraceful, with bickering, superficial women, coupled with a belief that the behavior seen in these shows adds too generously to the general, negative stereotypes about black folks. Sometimes, she's more sophisticated but looks like her wealth came from osmosis or a rich man. Some of their finely-appointed homes are rented for the window of production, and they're always eating out and having cocktails at the best venues. They also wear designer clothes straight off the runway, that is, if not boosted from their cousins who are in the shoplifting game. I generalize, but the point I'm trying to make is: what ends up in the finished cut is a wealthy, socially superior or social-climbing, "crazy lady" (sometimes) who is often part of a dysfunctional relationship, whether past or present, with a man being her source of financial gain.

Upon closer inspection, I see some creators making more effort to show a balance. *Married to Medicine*, for instance, Bravo's show with five seasons features women who are doctors, including a Spelman graduate, and their husbands, as well as women who are married to doctors. It's good TV, but there are still swearing matches and, from time to time, some physical drama. Bottom line, reality show stars are attention seekers who are willing to expose themselves and their families to millions of people. The generally low production cost of reality shows has led to an explosion in the number of unscripted cable programs featuring black women as "leading ladies."

Personally, I'm not drawn to these "real-life soap operas" for their antics, nor am I into the violence. Just like I could look past the suspended reality of an unbelievable soap opera plot, I can also look beyond the obvious manipulation that stimulates largely flamboyant responses in these stars. Sometimes it's the dramatic irony of knowing that a person is going to see someone that they aren't expecting to see for the first time. Other times, it's at an event that has an open bar, so you can predict bad behavior from at least one person in scenes like these. Unfortunately, the genre inherently shapes more minds to indulge in behavior that's unacceptable. I actually know people who, before the cameras started rolling, weren't those kind of people, but with fame and prodding, they became caricatures of themselves. I have seen folks come into reality centered and calm, and before it's done they are insecure and violent, talking about folks behind their backs, creating drama for the cameras, and finding their true relationships undone at the hands of such behavior.

I suspect reality is therapeutic for both the cast and audience. It certainly has been for me!

While casting directors do make every effort to cast strong personalities who are willing to push the envelope, the stories are, for the most part, real. Even where there may be pre-set scenarios and scripting involved, the "performances" are legitimate. Though scripted to some extent, the women maintain control over their language, gestures, etc., so we get a range of representations of black women. The range of programming adds to this as well.

The Real Housewives of Atlanta is a show that has aired on Bravo since 2008. These women have tackled everything from colorism in the black community to perceptions of class. They have reinforced some stereotypes while flipping others. Via the bullying, backstabbing, money-grubbing, and narcissism of this nouveau riche clique: wigs are snatched, names are dropped, and many, many arguments are had...

The addition of model Cynthia Bailey and Kandi Burress, a Grammy-winning songwriter and former member of R&B group Xscape, brought an earnest look at women's work lives (though this didn't overshadow the catfights).

I've had the chance to hang out with many of them over the years and, to me, they've always been on their best behavior. Some have tried to explain the behavior away by attributing it to the commands of producers and directors. In 2009, I got to see for myself what that world was like. I got in on the "reality game" as a producer for the Keyshia Cole spinoff with her mother and sister, Frankie and Neffe. It wasn't a crowning moment on my resume, but I got the opportunity to do some good work. First things first, having heard so much about these shows being scripted and fake, I didn't want to compromise my journalistic background and integrity to obtain freelance producing work inside a year where my main clients weren't up and running like usual. Still, upon closer inspection, I uncovered up-close that producers do outline the flow of these productions. But what happens can happen, and when it happens, you have to be able to go where it takes you. Working on *Frankie & Neffe*, for example, we never knew what we were going to get from Frankie because she might have been out all night partying and, as a result, may not have been ready to get up at the time we agreed we'd start shooting. Over time, I had to get creative on how we shot with Frankie to get her cooperation. She'd still cuss me out and throw almost-empty bottles of Tanqueray in my direction if she wasn't pleased. It was like a rather harsh form of babysitting. But, if we were patient, and fed her some context for what the scene was about, we'd get TV gold. Not the kind that I liked to watch, but the kind that had *Frankie & Neffe* become one of the top-rated reality shows of 2010.

With R&B songstress Monica, the ride was more to chronicle her comeback, so we just shot what was going on in her studio sessions, talent meetings, and photo shoots. I was proud that her show was also one of BET's top-rated docu-series without relying upon table throwing and unnecessary drama. Monica doesn't drink and she's the last drama queen. We got a charming view of her up close for the first time, as a mom with her cute sons and getting to see them bond. If we'd shot a second season, we would have gotten drama as she and her children's father Rocco broke up, which would have made for exciting TV. As I observed that there was little to no chemistry or demonstrative connection between Monica and Rocco, I thought them "doing a scene" on a date would hopefully open him up and reignite what seemed lacking to my naked eye. They agreed and enjoyed a meal at Kiko's Steakhouse in Buckhead. The scene didn't produce much heat of the loving or disagreeing kind, which made the intention of the scene a bust...

The reality genre now has something for everyone. During a location interview with Shaquille O'Neal and his family when he played for the Phoenix Suns, I remember his then-wife Shaunie telling me about her vision for what became *Basketball Wives*. I knew a show chronicling the wives, girlfriends, baby mamas and ex-wives (Shaunie now among them) of the super-rich and talented athletes would be a hit, and it was! Now the VH-1 show is a franchise in which Shaunie acts as a queen mother, steering away from the controversy and acting more as a moderator, leaving the infighting to some of her cast-mates like Evelyn Lozado (whose life was fixed by Iyanla), Jackie Christie and Tami Romain.

If you can't break a glass on *Love & Hip-Hop*, you're not invited to the party. Once-Missy-Elliott manager Mona Scott reinvented her brand and became a master TV producer of a franchise, which some argue saved VH1 from the wanton advertising sales blues in 2011. Enter *Love & Hip Hop: New York*, then its sizzling spin-offs in Atlanta, Hollywood, and Miami.

Reality TV continues to get pegged as reductive and fake. But the success of the genre as a format that continues to get greenlighted by the networkers shows that it's not going anywhere (though a return to scripted drama is giving reality a run for its money). What will sustain reality is inspiration. This type of TV that has made stars of out the Kardashians and the Real Housewives also has a pulse. Even with my understanding of the behind-the-scenes manipulations that can sometimes present themselves on location and the like, the messages are real. Often, the women featured in these real-life dramas are offering me authentic inspiration that can get me in step with my own life.

SCRAPBOOK

More than just the daughter of music legend Lionel Richie, Nicole Richie is an actress, author, and designer. She launched her signature jewelry line, House of Harlow 1960. In 2010, she added fashion into the mix via Winter Kate which launched worldwide in 2010. Nicole Murphy's career and life have taken on several changes. We first got to know her as a model—representing top brands including Ungaro, Chanel, Yves St. Laurent, and Valentino. At one step, she married Eddie Murphy, with whom she had five children. In 2009, after they divorced, she opened her own jewelry line called FLB by Nicole Murphy. Once engaged to Michael Strahan, she is most recently the star and executive producer of the reality series **Hollywood Exes**, a popular docu-series chronicling ex-wives of famous men.

Amidst Fashion Week, got to hang out with Nicole Richie at an event she hosted at Bergdorf Goodman February 2011. She was promoting her "About Winter Kate | House of Harlow 1960" line.

Harlem's Fashion Row 5th Anniversary gala for Mercedes-Benz Fashion Week at Jazz at Lincoln Center featured a celebrity model: Nicole Murphy. My friend Carl, who helped secure her, ensured I got some pose time with her.

Amber Rose was first known as a video vixen in some popular musical flicks, including Nicki Minaj's "Massive Attack" and Mary Mary's "God in Me." From the shadows of being "Kanye West's girlfriend" to having a child with Wiz Khalifa, Amber Rose now does her own thing—including a 2016 self-titled talk show on VH1. Additionally, she did the 23rd season of **Dancing with the Stars** and finished ninth.

With Amber Rose backstage September 2010 at Indashio's 2011 Collection at the Metropolitan Pavilion.

We may think we know Yandy Smith from VH1 reality TV series **Love & Hip Hop: New York**, but did you know that she was a Howard University graduate with a degree in Business Management? She has worked at Violator Management, Warner Bros music, and Monami Entertainment. Quite the entrepreneur, she has an accessories line, Everything Girls Love, that now exists as the jump of an entire lifestyle brand for women. Billboard Magazine recognized her in 2008 as one of its

"Top 30 Executives under 30" as she has managed many star clients including LL Cool J, 50 Cent, Missy Elliot and Busta Rhymes. After Mona Scott founded the television production company Monami Entertainment, Yandy was appointed its first president. After she met rapper Jim Jones while traveling on a private jet to Detroit for a hip-hop summit, she attracted another manager and brought more content to Monami and VH1—including **Love & Hip Hop: New York** and specials like **Love & Hip Hop Live: The Wedding**—chronicling Yandy's wedding to Mendeecees Harris.

Yandy Smith came by to give Arise Entertainment 360 the scoop on her nuptials to Mendeecees. May 2015. We'd all find out later that they weren't legally married.

We got to know more about Melyssa Ford—the person—in 2014, when Bravo introduced the docu-series **Blood, Sweat, & Heels**—in which her struggles as a realtor were chronicled as they documented the social life of New York City women.. But she's had more eyes on her throughout her career—dating back to the late 90s when music video director Little X discovered her while she was bartending at a Toronto nightclub. She catapulted into major success—appearing in film and TV projects, but most notably, music videos and men's magazines.

November 2011. Thurgood Marshall College Fund's 24th Anniversary Dinner at the Sheraton New York Hotel & Towers.

We know Jennifer Williams from **Basketball Wives** as the ex of professional basketball player Eric Williams. Along the way, she's pursued an array of entrepreneurial work – from real estate to clothing lines. Once (and recently) romantically linked to Tim Norman, son of Robbie Montgomery, the Sweetie Pie's restaurant founder out of St. Louis.

American Airlines announces Laz Alonso is new travel ambassador for BlackAtlas.com at Studio Museum in Harlem. August 2012.

Laura Govan is the ex-fiancée to NBA All-Star Basketball player Gilbert Arenas, known as popularly as Agent Zero. She became an immediate star on **Basketball Wives LA** – steering her life in the direction of enterprise from other TV appearance work such as **BV 365** of the Huff Post, **I Dream of Nene**, and **Iyanla: Fix My Life**. She also dabbles in children's books and design. Laura's sister, Gloria Govan also appeared on both **Basketball Wives** and **Basketball Wives: LA**.

Laura Govan is always in the right places. Here we are saying "Hi" at Michael Costello show during Fashion Week in February of 2015.

At Fashion Week event between the Govan sisters circa 2012.

Nene Leakes is probably the poster child for what a regular person does with their reality platform—to ensure their 15 minutes lasts a lifetime. We know her from **The Real Housewives of Atlanta**, but Nene is booked. She was Roz Washington on the Fox musical smash **Glee**, and played Rocky Rhoades as a series regular on the **The New Normal**, though it was canceled in 2013. Then, came major reality franchises like Donald Trump's **The Celebrity Apprentice** and ABC's **Dancing with the Stars**. She came to Broadway twice—first as Madame in Rodgers & Hammerstein's **Cinderella** in 2014, then in 2015 as Matron "Mama" Morton in **Chicago**. And on and on, we could go. She's even a stand-up comedian who takes her show on the road—from time to time.

With Nene at the EBONY 100 gala at Jazz at Lincoln Center, October 2011.

With Nene at the Michael Costello show during Fashion Week, February 2015.

From my days in Atlanta in the mid-to-late '90s, I stumbled into Kenya Moore as she was a Black Hollywood player—producing and starring in approachable fare. In the last handful of years, I saw her persona as a **Real Housewives of Atlanta** star. But I'll never forget 1993 when she rose to fame. She won Miss USA and even competed in Miss Universe—making it to the top six. She had a steady stream of Hollywood work after that—including small roles in films like **Waiting To Exhale** and **Deliver Us From Eva**. Since **Real Housewives of Atlanta**, she's become further popular in the reality realm—including **Celebrity Apprentice**.

Got to see Kenya Moore twirl at gay bar SPLASH when her **"Gone With The Wind Fabulous"** song came out Fall 2014.

Fun to pose alongside Kenya Moore at the Michael Costello Fashion Show during Fashion Week February 2015 in New York.

Modeling since she was a kid, America came to know Stacie J as a contestant on the second season of **The Apprentice** (before the Celebrity franchise took over). Out of that boardroom, she is the owner of a Subway franchise in Harlem across from President Clinton's office on 125th Street. Amidst spot modeling, acting, and community work, Stacie J raises her children quietly in Harlem.

Here **(above photo)** we are at Red Rooster in Harlem. April 2013—for the documentary **Free Angela: And All Political Prisoners**.

Stacie J, Sidra Smith, and I enjoyed Dance Theatre of Harlem's **Vision Gala** in April, 2013.

Gizelle Bryant blew up when Bravo introduced her to its audience as one of **The Real Housewives of Potomac**. But that zip code doesn't make a woman. She comes from father Curtis Graves, who was a high-ranking official at NASA for 30 years after being in the Texas House of Representatives in the late '60s. One of Gizelle's jobs after graduating Hampton University with a degree in marketing was working with the city council of Birmingham as a fundraiser for municipal improvements in order to raise money to improve the city. She also went on to become an events planner for the NAACP. Currently, she's planning her beauty takeover by launching her own makeup line, which is "geared to meet the needs of women of color."

In September 2017, I attended the Congressional Black Caucus. In a sea of influential people, panels, and productions, I had to take some time to stop by Gizelle's EveryHUE Beauty booth and say hello. We have a few friends in common. Also in the mix were her 'Potomac' colleagues Ashley Darby, Robyn Dixon, Karen Huger, Charrisse Jackson-Jordan and Monique Samuels.

From her early days as a television host at a local Tennessee news station, Mariah knew that to effectively tell a story, it needs to be sold to the right audience. Well, as the mastermind and producer behind the successful reality series **Married to Medicine**, the proof is certainly in the pudding. Blending beauty and brains, this strong, determined woman can light up a room. Whether she's busy blogging or cooking an Indian-Soul-food meal, this busy mother of two never neglects to add a sassy twist to everything she does. To top it off, Mariah is Chief Operating Officer (COO) of Jewel and Jem, the children's pajama and décor company she runs with her sister, Lake.

Mariah and Dr. Aiden from Married to Medicine were in the house for the Silver Celebration for Morehouse and Spelman! May 2017.

Omarosa gained fame as a contestant on the first season of Donald Trump's original American version of **The Apprentice,** then later **Celebrity Apprentice**... and she continues to be credited as one of TV's top villains in reality TV. Her most recent stint was **Celebrity Big Brother** after she got fired from the Trump Administration White House.

Ran into Omarosa at a Radio City Music Hall benefit. She recognized me from a mutual friend Paul Wharton, a TV personality and stylist out of DC.

chapter 11

The (Gay) Family

My dad, though a military man, was not a tough guy. Therefore, I didn't spend a lot of time with a complex about not being a kid of the rough and tumble kind. He never judged my behavior even if it seemed less than masculine. But I did have a brood-ish older brother named Herman and in his heterosexual little boy form, he made it clear that I was something different. I didn't always want to go outside and play ball. It was clear I had "stars" in my eyes as a presenter and singer. But little edits and notes on what boys were supposed to do were never too far from the dialogue. And the day I channeled my high-singing voice, eventually a falsetto, I was six years old. I was singing all of the songs by the female singers and Philip Bailey in Earth, Wind, & Fire. Lots of music and records! And my note always landed atop the four-part harmony when my big sister Janice, Herman and I did sibling talent shows. I got away with singing the cute, high notes that Michael Jackson or the Sylvers delivered. But I also snatched the really high notes my sister Janice couldn't hit, like Natalie Cole's "Our Love." Dad sometimes had my brother and me joining he and his brothers on some old school, quartet-style gospel.

My big brother, Herman, spent lots of time in my teen years wanting to know if I had a girlfriend or wanting to know who was the "girl" on the other line. Of course, that would be my brother's concern. If it wasn't that, he was calling me a "sissy" or a "faggot" for what he perceived were my effeminate ways. One day, it might have been that I wasn't outside playing with the boys and was inside reading a book about Diana Ross instead. Other times, it would be that I carried my backpack like a purse instead of a "backpack." Once in high school a girl named Rachel became my BFF and she still is to this day. But she became expectant for herself as well as my whole families' hope that maybe she might become a girlfriend.

By seventh grade, inquiring minds wanted to know who I was seeing. And whenever the question came up about whether or not I had a girlfriend, or whenever I needed to have a young lady on my arm, Rachel was there. And during that time, it was a real relationship and I truly did love her. I love her to this day. I loved us together even for how we functioned and interacted. But I now see that bond we shared provided just the right amount of connection and disconnection for me to not feel suffocated.

Rachel and I connected and stayed together through high school and some college. I was her escort and she was mine for all things including prom and the debutante ball. We always had a good time with fine dining, beach adventures and virgin daiquiris. I did love her and she was what would help me quiet the parts of me that felt I was gay but could never freely communicate it, ever. The South didn't make me feel that gayness was something anyone would want to "exclaim" proudly. And I had no role models to teach or encourage me otherwise.

There's still a dearth of black lesbian, gay, bisexual and transgender representation. At large, many still don't want to come out.

In *The Color Purple*, Celie is nudged by a bisexual named Shug Avery to come out to just her if not anyone else. From the lesbian cap of *The Color Purple* author, advocate and womanist Alice Walker as well as the iconic political scholar, Angela Davis, we now have the pleasure of knowing women who stand in their truth and their fluidity.

Though softened in the 1985 film adaptation of *The Color Purple* as a kiss and a flirtation, Walker finely details in her book that Celie and Shug are passionate lovers. Thus, offering a rounded out story about lesbians and bisexuals that had never been so explored and accepted in the lexicon.

Political activist Angela Davis announced her lesbian identity in an *OUT* magazine interview in 1997. She said she was reluctant to speak about her sexuality because of the stereotypes often placed on lesbians and that her work as a leader within the Black Panther Party was the most important focus. As the Black Panthers were a rare radical group that had women in the lead, Angela wanted no more distractions. After she became a political prisoner and a human rights icon and scholar, she felt strongly that those details would be a distraction. But she's out now!

Even as a child, I'd read about the fluid orientations of icons like blues singers Ma Rainey or Bessie Smith and international star Josephine Baker. Yet the information was always vague and reduced to a paragraph. As a kid, I could first hear the voice of the people I was around. If I read something like that around my mom, she might say "That's the devil." I'd counter, which is also my second internal thought. "Who are we to say who should love whom?" Usually, there was a biblical response. Most times though, the answer was more "Because I said so." My third thought, before I could reconcile what was going on inside of me, was "I wonder, are they more like me than not?" Then I'd land on how courageous they must have been to have lived their lives openly at that time. I prayed then for a day when I could be that free.

In recent times, at a petty pace, we see more out and proud LGBTQ people of color. I admire many of the women who are part of this community for being themselves and sharing their truths.

There are a couple who never cared if you knew they were gay like LaBelle legend, Nona Hendryx and singer/bassist Meshell Ndegeocello. Singer, Frenchie Davis sings it loud from the rafters, figuratively and literally speaking. She first came to our attention as the one to beat on season two of *American Idol*. The other women contestants were afraid to group up with her at risk of being drowned out by the Jennifer-Holliday-level voice with the bombastic body to go with it.

Kimberly Locke wasn't scared and would go on to third place just under Ruben Studdard and Clay Aiken. But Frenchie would be disqualified from the preliminaries and asked to return home after some suggestive pictures of her in lingerie were uncovered and appraised by production. The show continued on as Frenchie joined the cast of *Rent* on Broadway; traveled with the touring cast of *Dreamgirls* as Effie White and eventually finalized on *The Voice*. Her "Like a Prayer," originally by Madonna, was next level. Inside it all, Frenchie has stayed true to her bisexual self and continued to be a stand for LGBTQ causes. You can always count on Frenchie to wave the rainbow flag and I love her for it.

My girlfriend, Cy, who is a transgender woman let me be a part of her transition. Transgender advocate and actress, Laverne Cox, is a good friend of hers. She'd always tell my partner and me about her friend Laverne, who I finally got to meet at an Out 100 event. She was very much a star and lit up the room. Most know and adore her as Sophia Burset on the big Netflix hit *Orange Is the New Black*. She further opened the door for LGBTQ people as she was nominated for an acting Emmy Award. She was the first openly transgender person to receive the honor. The notoriety kept coming as Laverne became the first openly transgender woman to win a Daytime Emmy Award in 2015 as executive producer for her special, *Laverne Cox Presents: The T Word*.

And you can see her history-making wax figure at Madame Tussauds. Then she landed on the CBS show *Doubt*. She's come a long way since we first met her on the first season on VH1's, *I Want to Work for Diddy*. Transgender model, Isis King and gay New Orleans rapper, Big Freedia stand on the shoulders of Laverne along with activist Janet Mock.

Wanda Sykes has called being gay, African-American and a woman the "trifecta of discrimination" in Hollywood. She came out reluctantly in 2008. By then, she was a household name. She was first recognized for her work as a writer on *The Chris Rock Show*, for which she won a Primetime Emmy Award in 1999. In 2004, Entertainment

Weekly named Sykes as one of the 25 funniest people in America. She is also known for her role as Barb Baran on CBS' *The New Adventures of Old Christine* and for appearances on HBO's *Curb Your Enthusiasm*. Aside from her television appearances, Sykes has also had a career in film, appearing in *Monster-in-Law*, *My Super Ex-Girlfriend*, *Evan Almighty* and *License to Wed*.

Wanda publicly came out as a lesbian while she was at a same-sex marriage rally in Las Vegas, regarding Proposition 8. A month earlier, Sykes had married her partner Alex Niedbalski, a French woman, whom she had met in 2006. The couple also became parents on April 27, 2009, when Alex gave birth to a pair of fraternal twins, daughter Olivia Lou and son Lucas Claude. Sykes only came out to her conservative mother Marion and father Harry when she was 40, who both initially had difficulty accepting her homosexuality. They declined to attend her wedding with Alex, which led to a brief period of estrangement. They have since reconciled with Sykes and are now proud grandparents to the couple's children.

I stand on each and every one of these women's shoulders. And every time they say it's okay, I feel a little better about being out. Managing all of that internally in the late '70s and early '80s meant that, externally, I had to make it look another way. In my teen years and into my 20s, I spent a lot of time running from this truth inside me for the comfort of my homophobic loved ones, the bullies and the young ladies who were willing to look away from the obvious because of socialization. But by my mid-20s, I knew my experiment in alternative truths was no way to live. Through undeniable pain, I eventually found the courage to come out using the lyrics of one of my soul-spirit songwriting divas, Carole Bayer Sager on a hit tune by Miss Ross to seal the deal. The track is "It's My Turn," which starts: "I can't cover up my feelings in the name of love, or play it safe, for a while that was easy. And if living for myself is what I'm guilty of, go on and sentence me, I'll still be free..."

There were many coming outs to many important people in my life. It got me in touch with how far I can go, how far we have to go and how it's important to know your worth before you can manage your worth. Accepting my sexuality didn't happen overnight and it hasn't always been easy for me.

By 1998, in time for my ten-year high school reunion, I, gay and proud, was hired to work as a freelance senior field producer for *The Oprah Winfrey Show*. From time to time, my bosses would break the fourth wall and show me on-camera. These were moments that always excited my family down South. One assignment, though, took me right back to the resistance and homophobia that raised me. In 2005, my bosses at *The Oprah Winfrey Show* told me Miss Winfrey wanted me to testify in the segment "When I Knew I Was Gay." On this assignment, they'd already assigned me to interview a half-dozen or so folks on their stories and to bring some diversity to my batch of subjects. They asked if I'd turn the camera on myself. Well, easier said than done. (I mentioned I'm from the Bible Belt, right?) But I agreed, with butterflies in my stomach through it all. I knew that what was going to have to come out of me was the truth and that perhaps my loved ones wouldn't want to hear it. But I answered each question the interviewer asked of me. The main question was: "When Did You Know You Were Gay?" I referenced 1978 as the year because I felt informed enough internally to think that it might be that. "I always felt different than other boys since age 3 or 4." I added. "I always sort of found myself drawn to the women in my life: my mom, my sister, Diana Ross...." I would go on to talk about a number of other deep things, including my family's take on other gays. I didn't know to call it homophobia but I felt a certain kind of way every time my big brother opened his mouth to make fun of an effeminate man on the street, primarily behind his back. What landed in the televised edit was an anecdote I shared about Diana Ross. "There were many times as a child that, behind closed doors, I'd be playing my Diana music at the highest volume." I reflected. "Before it was all said and done, I'd be on my figurative heels, with maybe even a towel on my head, singing "I'm Coming Out!" It's a real recollection. The producers found it cute and inviting.

Another anecdote considered from my interview was about my adoration of Debbie Allen and *Fame*. I wanted to be in Lydia Grant's dance class and work those numbers like her star student Leroy did every time it was his turn in the spotlight. Those high kicks and window-to-the-wall flourishes inspired me to spend lots of time hopping from couch to fireplace to coffee table. I wanted to be a dancer. Generally speaking, the sentiment from my nuclear world was that dancing was for sissies. By this time, all I needed to hear was the word "sissy" or "faggot," and I would let my associated dreams dissipate.

As soon as I completed the interview, I felt limp and drained. Though it was good to share the special and honest memories. I felt like the recollections would be embarrassing to my family. But I said the words and I meant them. And that's all there would be.

After the show aired, you could hear a pin drop. I was so used to people calling during the show and right after when I'd be on, it was hurtful, yet no surprise, that I didn't hear a peep from Georgia. But let me tell you how this choice resulted in my growth.

Despite resistance from my nearest and dearest at home, that show, and our producing team at The Oprah Winfrey Show, won a GLAAD Award. That's the Gay & Lesbian Alliance Against Defamation! Major! And since that time, I continue to run into young and old LGBTQ people who thank me for what some have called my "life-saving" testimonial because, as seen in one quote from a fan I bumped into outside The Color Purple theater in 2005, "You let me know I was not alone!!!"

SCRAPBOOK

Hampton University grad, Wanda Sykes took her funny from the college campus to the stage. And today, she is known by many as one of the funniest women in America. We first came to know her in the late '90s as a writer for **The Chris Rock Show** for which she won an Emmy Award for her writing. After years of stand up and comedy writing, Wanda became a comic actress. Early on she appeared in Chris Rock's offerings including **Down to Earth** and **Pootie Tang**. Later she played Barbara Baran on **The New Adventures of Old Christine** opposite Julia Louis Dreyfus. She came out as lesbian to the public in 2008 and has been a vocal gay rights supporter. She's married and has two kids.

While at Janet Jackson Radio City Music Hall show in spring 2013, Wanda Sykes happened to be seated a few seats down in the same row. She was gracious as she exited the aisle to leave before Janet's encore. GASP! The nerve! LOL!

When Laverne Cox saw Candis Cayne premiere on ABC's primetime series **Dirty Sexy Money** in 2007, she knew it was possible to be openly trans and have a career as an actress. The next year, she booked her first appearance on an episode of **Law and Order**. Then a second **Law and Order** appearance. She then did her first pilot for HBO's **Bored To Death**, followed by a reality show called **I Wanna Work for Diddy** which lead to her producing and starring in her first show on VH1 called **TRANSform Me**. In 2012 she booked the show that would change her life, **Orange is the New Black**—making her the first trans woman of color to have a leading role on a mainstream, scripted TV show. She is Emmy-nominated now and she's turned her platform into opportunity for others in the business as she is an award-winning documentary film producer and an equal rights advocate. Laverne Cox continues to make history in her career and significant strides in her activism. She's much decorated, including a SAG Award for "Outstanding Performance by an Ensemble in a Comedy Series."

November 2013 brought many out to Terminal 5 for OUT 100 – including Debbie Harry who performed her Blondie classics. Laverne Cox presented this night, but when not on the stage, she mingled with everyone very humbly. It was lovely to meet her.

Gail Marquis is a world class athlete who, as a pro basketball player, won a silver medal in the 1976 Montreal Olympics. She has been inducted into the New York City Basketball Hall of Fame. Audrey Smaltz is a former model and is the Founder & CEO of the Ground Crew, a company that specializes in managing backstage at fashion shows and other live industry events. They met taking a self-improvement class. Audrey was not gay but desired a relationship. Gail was gay and not sure if Audrey was or not. They found love in each other and got married November 2011.

At OUT 100 event November 2013, Gail Marquis and her wife Audrey Smaltz were honored for their example individually and collectively. I was proud to toast them that night.

Angela Robinson Whitehurst plays homophobic Veronica Hamilton on Tyler Perry's **The Haves & The Have Nots** on the Oprah Winfrey Network. But Angela Robinson Whitehurst is the total opposite. She's LGBTQIA affirming and considers us family, she told one LGBTQIA group that was honoring her for her example. Angela is the 2015 recipient of the Gracie Award for a role in the film **One to Watch**. She's worked on a host of stages globally, stateside and on Broadway. Among my highlights: **The Color Purple** with Fantasia, **Wonderful Town**, **Bells Are Ringing**, and **Play On**! Angela is a devoted member of the Grammy Nominated Broadway Inspirational Voices. Angela and her husband, Scott, founded the White Robin Group in 2008. A consulting firm for aspiring and seasoned artists. Providing training, inspiration and direction via acting workshops, private acting coaching, blogs and mentorship programs.

Spring 2012, at The Broadway Inspirational Voices concert, Angela Robinson Whitehurst is a member of the choir. Her show **The Haves & The Have Nots** had just begun to air on the Oprah Winfrey Network. Everyone was excited to greet her and congratulate her.

Memorial Day Weekend 2017, at XSCAPE Puerto Rico 2017.

LGBTQ music and arts festival for which I was a Brand Ambassador and Host of The Vanguard Awards which honored Angela with an award.

chapter 12

Singers

Singing is the one thing this country has always allowed black people to do. When we weren't allowed to read, we could sing. When emotions had to be tempered down or messages transported, song was our medium. Every black person knows whether or not they can sing. Between gospel churches and carport singing groups, the pool of talented black singers is wide and deep so if you make it through, you can REALLY sing.

We have a special relationship with music. We created gospel, jazz, and blues which stand on the shoulders of the Negro spirituals and slave songs that preceded them.

I came out of the womb hearing song, it seems. Of course, it's in my DNA via mom and dad, likely as soon as my ears and hearing took shape. And my earliest memories are of hearing singing and harmonizing in the house between my dad and his singing buddies. It was either his childhood friends from Savannah or fellow military men who enjoyed vocalizing. My first connection to my falsetto is from my dad as he would put on songs like The Swan Silvertones "He's Sweet I Know" and "Walk Around Heaven All Day" by the Mighty Clouds of Joy. Certainly, I identify Eddie Kendricks, Philip Bailey, and in more recent years, Bobby and El Debarge, as well as Maxwell as my inspirations for using the head voice. But Paul Beasley, who joined the legendary Mighty Clouds of Joy in the '70s, made these gospel giants even bigger for me as he waxed nostalgically-on-high beautiful spiritual ballad "Walk Around Heaven All Day." I just loved that song. My sensitivity also took the song as one of the lyrics is "My mother will be waiting and my father too...." Dad is still with me, but mom left in 1994. I would shiver at that lyric then despite the beauty of the notes.

Powerhouse vocalist Patti LaBelle would remake "Walk Around Heaven All Day" on her album, *The Gospel According to Patti LaBelle* as an indication of the chops required to sing this big song. And in addition to my iconic divas, I've always had an ear for the range of voices that came from women. So, I sang this one a lot for sure. Perhaps in the household, I can remember also awakening to the sounds of the Caravans which eventually roster changed to include gospel great Albertina Walker. At their peak, as a group in the 1950s, the high-volume and gymnastic mezzo-soprano Shirley Caesar and the bombastic contralto Inez Andrews brought the soundtrack of my Sunday mornings throughout childhood and whenever I find my way to my childhood home.

Though he was a male artist, I had an instinct that there was something special about Luther Vandross. Sure, I read that his three favorite divas were Dionne Warwick, Aretha Franklin and Diana Ross. That news made me know he was one of mine. I'd later on learn that many treats to my ear were attributable to him before I started reading liner notes. He was featured prominently on the *Young Americans*, refrain of the androgynous David Bowie's album of blue-eyed soul from 1975. By 1978, when I was reading the credits, I found out that he co-wrote one of my favorites from *The Wiz*, "Can You Feel A, Brand New Day?" along with my other favourite composers, Ashford & Simpson. Then my young journalist research would lead me to the fact that he was the king of the commercial jingles including my jams from Kentucky Fried Chicken, Juicy Fruit and State Farm. And once he transitioned from another group change, the tunes of which I recognized like "Glow of Love" and "Searching," I just knew that his solo material was going to be off the charts. And it was! I loved every song he released from "Never Too Much" to his Dionne Warwick remake of "A House is Not a Home" to "Bad Boy Having a Party," to his Stevie Wonder/Aretha Franklin mash-up "Until You Come Back To Me"/"Superstar." Moreover, he got the chance to produce his divas. He produced three Arista albums between Aretha Franklin and Dionne Warwick, garnering R&B hits like "Jump to It" and "Get It Right" for the Queen of Soul. And for Whitney's cousin Dionne who was due another hit, they released a duet called "How Many Times Can We Say Goodbye?" Even Miss Ross gave Luther a couple of chances to produce her backgrounds including a '50s doo-wop-sounding number she wrote and produced called "So Close." This followed the *Silk Electric* album's lead-off hit, the Grammy-nominated "Muscles" written and produced by Michael Jackson. Additionally, in 1987, he'd write and produce a full song for Diana. A ballad called "It's Hard for Me to Say," that he himself would remake in 1991 on his *Secret Love* album. Diana brought that song back when she appeared on *The Oprah Winfrey Show* for the last time making it a seated and sung tribute to Oprah. The fan favorite has now been added back into her show from time to time since that 2012 appearance.

One last Luther note: He was such a master of vocal arrangement, having worked his vocals behind Roberta Flack and Bette Midler. His sessions singers were, and still are the best including Cissy Houston, Tawatha Agee of Mtumes "Juicy Fruit" fame, Grammy-award-winning Lisa Fischer, Patti Austin, Fonzi Thornton and more.

As I would mature and learn more about favorite male singer Luther Vandross reported struggles with love, relationships and what many of his closest friends have articulated as a struggle with his sexual orientation, I sometimes felt like Luther. He was the No. 1 session singer in the '70s, and soon began to channel the vocalist well beyond the melodies of his string of hits. When he said, "She'll come into my life" at the end of his 1988 hit "Any Love" after declaring that non-discriminating sentiment, my thoughts were Luther's "any love" was a man. But despite what may or may not have been going on inside of Luther before he had a stroke and eventually passed away, the weight of people's lean on him for astounding vocals, hits and more baby making music was quite the irony considering he couldn't be his true self in public or have the full embodiment of unconditional love to which he hinted in his lyrics. Indeed, the Creator used many of the same ingredients in Luther as me, a touch of romance, too much sensitivity, loads of love, lots of longing, pockets of sadness, appreciation of beauty, grasp of melody, and wherever possible, never-too-distant joy. And by all measure, Luther looked to his singing divas for inspiration and collaboration, as I do.

Outside of our sibling rivalry, my brother and I actually created a singing group from 1975-1978 during our Air Force days in San Bernadino, California. We were PHD Incorporated, as in Patrick, Herman and Derrick. Derrick and his family lived down the street from us in base housing. After Derrick's father got relocated to another country, another Derrick came into town and we did a Florence-Ballard-Supremes-style replacement a la Cindy Birdsong. Remember when Motown's hottest trio had a roster change? My lead song was "Easy" by the Commodores. I also had the high part on "Boogie Fever." My brother Herman did "Let's Just Kiss & Say Goodbye." We were good. Or thought we were, with mom's styling and my sister's choreography. I guess we tried to work together but our lives moved in different directions.

After going "solo" in middle school and high school, I had to adapt Peter Brady-style, to an adolescent voice change that landed me on tones the likes of Jeffrey Osborne and Al Jarreau, both of whom navigated brilliantly between there lower tones and their falsettos. My Windsor Forest High School Show choir director Mary Sue Reagan would bless me with a solo of Jarreau's "Moonlighting" that I would get to perform solo. We rated high in all of our city-, county and statewide competitions. But the influence of women was never too far. I sang Barbra Streisand's "The Way We Were" for the senior banquet in Spring of 1988. Though Barbra's rendition was enough, I pulled from Gladys Knight & The Pips rendition which so happened to include "Try to Remember" in its medley form. "Try to Remember" is a big hit song from the Off-Broadway musical *The Fantasticks*, in which I also starred senior year in high school. The full circles around my favorite women singers continued in all steps of my life's trajectory.

I was blessed to have studied more about music once I got to Morehouse. More than what dad's gargantuan album collection of amazing music brought, my college classes were going to the root. We've been blending genres since the first Africans of different ethnic groups were transported to this country. Between providing free labor to plantations, enslaved people cultivated their own musical styles which would evolve into gospel, blues and what is now known as bluegrass and country music. Even after instruments of the enslaved were forbidden after the discovery of our ability to send messages through drums, we used our bodies and our voices to create music.

The world-renowned Morehouse College Glee Club was one of my extracurricular choices that got me serious about singing. We toured the country several times during my matriculation in college, performing a range of African songs, Negro spirituals, classical Voice, gospel and more. I not only enjoyed the exercise of rehearsing vocals and music in an academic setting but Mr. Morrow, now Dr., did not play. Gesturing for us to stay on pitch as his thumb massaged the tips of his pinky and its adjacent finger is an image that keeps me on key until this day. When people say I have perfect pitch, which I don't always have, I think of Mr. Morrow and the extensive vocal training in the Morehouse College Glee Club. I was excited to learn the discipline of breathing and how to take care of my voice. The glee club attracted a booking my way. When we were invited to Washington, D.C. to surprise Atlanta Symphony Orchestra, Chorus Composer and Conductor Robert Shaw, the Kennedy Center Honors producers chose me to deliver the speech that preceded our performance of "Betelehemu" a Nigerian Christmas song. "This song screams to a city of wonder." I explained to a room with faces in it like my favorite skit comedy actress Carol Burnett and CBS News icon Walter Cronkite. "Bethlehem... We thank you." This was a career moment before the first semester of my senior year in college, all because I sing.

Since college, I've continued the road of sidelight singing, channeling the catalogs and the nuances of my favorite women along the way. Singing at the weddings of many co-workers, bosses, friends and siblings friends. Maybe even a divorce ceremony or two. Eventually I took on the cabaret circuit and would performer every other month or so in popular but small cabaret rooms, such as Don't Tell Mama, the Duplex and the Bitter End. Mostly I billed my set "An Evening with Patrick L. Riley." I was accompanied by a rhythm section of piano, bass and drums. And I'd do a range of my favorite songs from all my divas.

Early on, my favorite singers ranged from Donna Summer to the Emotions, with their sweet melodies. In addition to their own litany of hits, this trio of sisters bring the air and the effervescence to the background of Earth, Wind & Fire's "Boogie Wonderland." Turns me on every time and you know I was singing along. I also recall Cheryl Lynn's "Shake It Up Tonight," "Encore" and "To Be Real." Those were my songs. In my shows, you'd for sure hear some Luther, Cheryl and Earth, Wind & Fire.

As more of my generation wanted their MTV in the 1980s, I kept up and partook of that menu as well. This included Cyndi Lauper in my repertoire from "Time After Time" to "True Colors," but I grew to absolutely love R&B and soul music during this time. Though I continued to love and sing everything from Whitney Houston to Diana Ross, there were many other tiers of singer who I adored during this time. One great in particular among many but who I'm certain won't even get an *Unsung: Cheryl "Pepsii" Riley*, whose 1988 debut single "Thanks for my Child," would wake me up every morning on our local R&B station E-93. There was little in the lyric that moved me as I didn't want children and still don't. But Cheryl's brand of sweet soul, produced by the Full Force, was nonetheless a favorite.

By 2008, I wasn't just in good enough professional standing to connect with my main divas but the work I've done as a pop culture expert and entertainment blogger has placed me as a go-to interviewer. I was too excited when Cheryl Pepsii Riley's publicist asked me if I'd interview her. I hadn't known that she'd done anything since that special song from my teen years but would soon find out that she'd been busy. She'd been starring in Tyler Perry's stage plays, including *Madea's Class Reunion* and *Why Did I Get Married?* When she and I met up at Mo-Bay Uptown Restaurant for a meal of fried chicken, catfish, collard greens and macaroni & cheese, I was moved by how fit and cute she was. Just like her album covers from back in the day. She and I had dimples in common and at a time where open mics were becoming less the norm in the city, Cheryl was and still is hosting a popular Monday night jam session at Village Underground that brought out all the great singers, either on the come up or rolling through town. In addition to her Tyler Perry plays, she now sings in his films. She did all of the vocals for Taraji P. Henson's character in Tyler Perry's *I Can Do Bad All by Myself* in 2009. And she does all of this as a stepmother, aunt of several grown kids and a grand aunt.

Even when we're not hearing from people via the radio or music channels, the real singers continue to sing no matter what. Jennifer Hudson may have gotten the boot prematurely from *American Idol* but she continued to sing. And what she attracted because she continued is bigger than a flimsy record deal.

After Fantasia and a slew of others auditioned to be the disgruntled but redeemed Effie White, the *Dreamgirls* character that gets to sing the blockbuster hit, "And I Am Telling You I'm Not Going," *American Idol* finalist Jennifer Hudson's name was thrown into the mix. When I interviewed her in Summer 2006 at the National Association of Black Journalists convention, she said she was turned down three times before ultimately getting yet another call from the producers that she won the role. Of course, she'd go on to win an Oscar for her Jennifer Holliday 2.0 rendition of "And I Am Telling You I'm Not Going." During our time together, a few months before the film's release, she sang three songs including "One Night Only" and a new ditty, "I Love You I Do" that was written just for the film. She also sang three other original tunes. I joked "I need a cigarette," after we saw a 30-minute teaser of the film and after Jennifer Hudson performed. Moreover, because Jennifer was embargoed from singing the big song from the movie to our group, I played with that restriction and decided to sing it myself. As I finished the last chorus and took the last breath after "You're gonna love..." Jennifer couldn't resist chiming in with me for the finish. "Me!!!!!" A standing ovation erupted, and Jennifer and I dropped the mic.

Often overlooked and underrated, Canadian R&B/soul musicians don't always get as much notoriety as they should. Still, I want to highlight two of my favorites who I feel don't get the right attention: Tamia and Deborah Cox, two stellar singers. They each had a moment or few at the top of the charts, but that frequency of commercial success escaped them.

Everyone knows who Tamia is. The Canadian-born singer/songwriter has been on the musical scene since 1995. I met her as my dear girlfriend Chandra was the assistant to the publicist Juanita Stephens for Tamia's mentor Quincy Jones' label Qwest. Her self-titled album *Tamia* might as well have been Michael Jackson's "Thriller" or "Off The Wall" because Quincy Jones was there the entire way. He outsourced for production support, as he does. Tamia's producing team included Mario Winans, Jermaine Dupri and Tim & Bob. The lead-off single from a prior Quincy collection, "You Put A Move On My Heart," was nominated for a Grammy. Her iconography and good looks were off the charts. She was nice and not scandalous, but it wasn't a big hit. She didn't give up. In fact, she kept singing, landing a spot on the classic diva collaboration "Missing You" featuring Gladys Knight, Brandy and Chaka Khan. That record gave her the first major hit and also another Grammy nomination. Then her album *A Nu Day* hit with her signature song "Stranger In My House" which doubled as a ballad and a dance hit. I love and sing both versions. The album featured production from Dallas Austin, Shep Crawford, Missy Elliott and Jazz Nixon. This was her first album on Elektra Records under powerbroker Sylvia Rhone. Missy was the biggest contributor on this album.

After that album, there was the feeling that things had slowed down. She'd had numerous releases, several of which included songs I adore but major label backing was a growing issue. She's done independent and even a return to a major Def Jam yet finds further chart success evading her. But her live performances continue to be brilliant, her following loyal and always excited to see her. I go to her shows whenever she's in town and I got to interview her promoting her fun single "Sandwich & a Cola." On social media, she said she loved our interview. I did too, after I looked at it on playback. I was very much the fan, palpitating inside at the excitement of interviewing my girl, Tamia.

I was cooler when I met Deborah Cox in 2013 at the Copacabana for the opening night party of Broadway's, *Trip to Bountiful*, the show starring Cicely Tyson in her Tony-award-winning turn. She was so gracious and excited to see me excited to see her. I told her that her 1998 release, *One Wish*, is one of my absolute favorites. I recalled for her a time in 1999 when my childhood friend Ernest, his sister Sam, a friend named Crystal and I were doing a New Year's Eve road trip from New York City to Buffalo, stumbling into a blizzard. Ern was driving and doing his due diligence to get us to destination safely. Meanwhile, to calm my nerves and because I just couldn't resist this project at the time, I was singing these songs at the top of my longs. Starting with the big hits "Nobody's Supposed To Be Here" and another favorite, "We Can't Be Friends." Deborah has later continued her work on the stage from Broadway's *Aida* to her most recent work in the touring musical *The Bodyguard*, an adaptation from the blockbuster film starring Whitney Houston. Deborah still records amazing dance songs that play to great success, even topping the Billboard dance charts in recent years. But for those who don't know, she is still in the best form.

The voices I admired growing up and continue to admire, are good voices but on some of my favorites, the vocals have depreciated and I'm empathetic. Smoking and drugs have ruined many of the best voices out there. Partying and not getting the right kind of rest can dehydrate and impact the voice of a pro. My heart breaks for the first time the amazing Whitney Houston didn't hit that note. And to see that it got worse over the years just made me cry. I continue to cry for the loss of Whitney and her voice. I still cry for the beauty that is the legacy of her recordings.

But for every disappointment, there are many greats from on high like Aretha, Diana, Patti and Gladys who are still in fine form. I hope folks are hearing what's happening with some of the younger crop who are also singing for their life including Jazmine Sullivan, Fantasia, Frenchie Davis, Kimberly Locke and more.

And the women I've just mentioned such as Cheryl Pepsii Riley, Jennifer Hudson, Tamia and Deborah Cox, are the best of the best. Despite a chart showing or whatever the stage, each of these women delivers every time. They speak of their regimens to stay healthy and ready. And though Jennifer Hudson's popularity is huge, that she doesn't sell music as well as other artists will not be a factor in hurting her career because she's such a pro. And her care and compassion for singers on the come up, most recently demonstrated by her winning turn on *The Voice UK* and her subsequent stint on *The Voice US*, runs deep. She's not keeping all the success for herself. As Jennifer Hudson mentors, Tamia and Deborah aren't just booked. They each contribute meaningful and palpable time to their LGBTQ following. I have seen them both deliver their goods at Pride events all over the nation. Like Jennifer Hudson but on a different stage, Cheryl, perhaps the least known of this batch is doing the work to ensure that our future generation of singers get to go and cut their teeth on live performances in front of New York City audiences.

All of these women sing because they are happy, I bet. And they sing wherever and to whomever because it comes from their hearts. It's their calling, they make me happy and their serenading watches over me.

SCRAPBOOK

This opera Diva Jessye Norman is the recipient of the Grammy Lifetime Achievement Award, the National Medal of Arts and has been inducted into the British Royal Academy of Music. She hails humbly from Augusta Georgia and is also in the Georgia Music Hall of Fame. Her dramatic soprano has been heard on many compositions, most notably the Wagnerian repertoire with the roles of Sieglinde, Ariadne, and others.

Opera Diva Jessye Norman at Dance Theater of Harlem gala. March 2013.

Three-time GRAMMY award-winning singer-songwriter Jill Scott at the premiere of Tyler Perry's **Why Did I Get Married** at the Bryant Park hotel on October 9, 2007 in New York City.

Jill Scott at the Steel Magnolias premiere in September 2012. The Paris Theatre.

Jill Scott at the premiere of Tyler Perry's **Why Did I Get Married 2** in New York City.

In 2003, Kimberly Locke was in third place on **American Idol**, the season. Ruben Studdard, The Velvet Teddy Bear, won. She's gone on to have a wonderful recording career. Also, she's become a fitness/nutrition/lifestyle expert and personality.

August 2010 at the National Association of Black Journalists Convention in San Diego. I was hosting a Disney presentation that featured American Idol finalist Kimberly Locke. We'd just done the Electric Slide or what some call, The Bus Stop.

Estelle hails from West London, England but splashed on the US charts with her single "American Boy" featuring Kanye West. Estelle continues to be known for her unique merging of dance, hip hop, reggae and R&B. Included in that stew are a range of collaborators like Rick Ross, Chris Brown, will.i.am and Robin Thicke. She has released several projects and received a Grammy Award among other accolades.

Hosting the Opening Night of the American Stroke Association event that she headlined. April 2011. The Apollo.

Plucked from Liverpool, England, Marsha Ambrosius embarked on her musical career as a member of Floetry. Ambrosius later released her debut solo album, **Late Nights & Early Mornings** in March 2011.

In New York City's Chelsea section of town at Club Splash to see Marsha Ambrosius show, promoting her solo debut Late Nights & Early Mornings.

Canadian born Deborah Cox is one of my favorite singers. Makes sense that Whitney Houston's, Svengali Clive Davis signed her as well. She's had quite the string of hits including a dozen #1 songs on Billboard's Hot Dance Club Play chart. In 2000, Cox collaborated with Whitney Houston to record the duet "Same Script Different Cast" for Houston's Greatest Hits CD. Deborah also does extensive stage work. She had a lead role in the Broadway debut in Elton John and Tim Rice's musical, **Aïda**. She most recently starred on Broadway in 2013 as Lucy in **Jekyll & Hyde**, and as the legendary Josephine Baker in **Josephine** at Asolo Repertory Theatre in April of 2016. Most recently, she's starring in **The Bodyguard** musical that is traveling all over the U.S. With her platinum selling debut album, Deborah Cox earned her an American Music Award nomination.

Deborah Cox and I sat near each other for the Broadway opening night of **The Trip To Bountiful**. We got to catch up at the After Party at the Copacabana nightclub. April 2013.

Keyshia Cole started as a kid with the mentoring of MC Hammer and Tupac Shakur, both of whom she as a teen. Tupac asked her to write a hook for one of his upcoming projects on the same night he passed away. At 21, she was signed to a record deal so she moved to Los Angeles from Northern California. In 2002, A&M Records released "Love," which would become her first platinum single. She's been nominated for a Grammy Award four times. She's also won several other awards including BET Awards, Soul Train Music Awards and an American Music Award. She did one season of **Love & Hip Hop: Hollywood** but she was one of the first to have her own show franchise. She appeared in three other reality television series that were centered on her life, including **Keyshia Cole: The Way It Is** from 2006-2008, **Keyshia & Daniel: Family First** in 2012, and **Keyshia Cole: All In** in 2015.

At the Premiere Party to celebrate Keyshia Cole's second reality show **Family First**, September 2012. Bevy Smith invited us to "Geffen/Interscope Presents "Cocktails W/Bevy" in honor of **Keyshia Cole: Woman To Woman**. Also, it was great to see so many of my FAB journalism and society friend's poolside at Jimmy's at The James Hotel in SOHO.

K. Michelle has been on the recording scene since 2009. Come 2012, she was added to the cast of VH1's reality series **Love & Hip Hop: Atlanta**. Appearing on the show led her to signing with Atlantic Records and releasing her long-awaited debut album, **Rebellious Soul**, to major success.

August 2013. K Michelle at G Lounge for a CD signing event.

Fantasia Barrino became the American Idol in 2004. The North Carolina native was thrust into the spotlight starting with the release of her debut album, Free Yourself. It and most of her recordings since have been well-received, if not a smash hit. Fantasia found renewed success as Celie on Broadway in **The Color Purple** from 2007 to 2008. She's tried reality, been married a couple of times and had some family drama. But what's consistent? Her singing voice and her willingness to go on the road and leave it all on the stage, city-by-city.

June 2009. Fantasia. LA LGBTQ Pride.

Avery Sunshine is a singer, songwriter, keyboardist, a Spelman College graduate as well as a wife and a mother. She is a native of Chester, PA where the church was her home away from home between singing in church and leading and directing the choirs. In 2005, she was hired to be the lead keyboardist for Tyler Perry's stage play **Meet The Browns** and in 2007 she was sought out by the first Effie White, Jennifer Holiday to be choral director for the **Dreamgirls** revival during the National Black Arts Festival in Atlanta. Now that she's a touring recording artist, her fan base continues to grow.

Avery Sunshine is a Spelman grad whose amazing vocals and musical prowess were commanded by the Queen of Soul for her birthday party.

When singer Joi Gilliam came out in the early 1990s, many were amused but not enough for her to have the commercial success she deserved. Still, over the last 25 years her cult audience and cutting-edge listeners are always waiting on her for what's new. Her Dallas, Austin produced, EMI label album debut, **The Pendulum Vibe**, was an eclectic and soulful mix of hip hop and funk. She would go on major tracks by Outkast and Goodie Mob from which she married Big Gipp for a time.

Two more releases were critically acclaimed but didn't get to the masses. During the 2000s, Joi replaced En Vogue's Dawn Robinson after she exited Lucy Pearl. And she has continued to sing live and record. The shows continue to be sold out by her following.

Joi Gilliam at the Apollo Music Café after her performance at The Apollo. February 12, 2011.

After many tries, Macy Gray wasn't sure she'd make it out of Canton, Ohio to do what she wanted to do, sing. But April 1998 came around and she landed a record deal with Epic and within two months of signing, Macy was at work on her debut CD on How Life Is. Released a year later, the album won over both the public and critics alike. The single "I Try" was huge. She continues to record and wow with her unique texture of vocal. Hollywood eventually came calling and she's landed roles in several films including **Training Day, Spider-Man**, and Tyler Perry's **For Colored Girls**.

Macy Gray's 18-year-old daughter Aanisah Hinds presented her art at the Harlem Art Crawl for which I was a host. Her venue to exhibit inside the four-gallery tour titled "Motown to Def Jam" was Strivers Row Gallery. The painting **But I'm Golden** is of her younger sister submitted as a tribute to Phyllis Hyman's song "The Kids."

I've known her since her days at WEA/QWEST after Quincy signed her to record her Grammy-winning "You Put a Move on My Heart." I got to catch up with her at the Ronald McDonald House in 2008 and I also got see her amazing show at the Highline Ballroom.

I interviewed Tamia at Arise Entertainment 360 Spring 2015.

SINGERS | 241

Melba Moore was a Young'n at Oprah's Legends Ball weekend in 2005 but by then, she was a legend. In 1968, she started singing background on Frank Sinatra and Aretha Franklin tracks. From that work came an invitation to do the Broadway musical, **Hair**, the same year. In 1969, she took over the lead part from Diane Keaton then, came more Broadway. First, her Tony Award-winning role in **Purlie**. Moore formed Hush Productions with her then-husband. Their first artist was R&B artist, Freddie Jackson. That same year, she released her Grammy-nominated, debut album entitled **Peach Melba**. Throughout the 1980s, Moore continued to record, release R&B hits and make appearances in all media including Ellis Island.

Hanging out with Melba Moore at Ernie Hanes Art Exhibit. Jazz at Lincoln Center. Fall 2007.

Melba Moore and Rhonda Ross joined me backstage so we could greet the Bold Soul Sisters who were featured in a live conversation at The Apollo. It featured Rochelle Fleming of First Choice, Nona Hendryx of Labelle, Ruth Pointer of The Pointer Sisters and Kathy Sledge of Sister Sledge. They talked about being women in the industry and the many trials they pushed through to entertain their fans and to make a living the way they know how.

I was a fan of Monica from the beginning. I moved to NYC in 1995 and saw her in 1995 at the Preachers Wife premiere. In 2009, I had the opportunity to produce Keyshia Cole's spin-off and worked some with Monica. Monica grew up in College Park, Ga. When she was 10 she became the youngest member of Charles Thompson and the Majestics, a traveling gospel choir. Honing her performance muscles in her teens registering for local talent shows would have her win upwards of 20 contests. In fact, Dallas, Austin discovered her at one of those showcases offering her a deal with his label, Rowdy Records. Her debut album, **Miss Thang**, was a major hit with several hit singles off of it. Two of the hit singles, "Don't Take It Personal; Just One of Dem Days" and "Before You Walk Out of My Life," made her the youngest artist ever to have two consecutive No. 1's on the R&B Singles chart. Miss Thang was Billboard Music Award winning and sold three million copies. Her BET reality show **Monica: Still Standing** which documented her personal life and the making of her album, **Still Standing**.

Monica at a pre-show meet-and-greet at Mist Harlem.

Brandy came on the scene as Thea's daughter on the short-lived sitcom in 1994. Once her music was ready to go, Atlantic Records released her self-titled debut album which produced back-to-back No. 1s "I Wanna Be Down" and "Baby." Brandy sold four million copies. In 1996, Brandy contributed to the Waiting to Exhale soundtrack recording "Sittin' up in My Room." Then came her return to TV, but in the lead; Moesha. That was a big success and the hits kept coming as she expanded her acting opportunities to include an eventful turn as Cinderella with Whitney Houston as her Fairy Godmother and a feature film **I Still Know What You Did Last Summer**. In 1998, she co-starred with Diana Ross as her mom in Double Platinum. She continues to act and sing.

244 | THAT'S WHAT FRIENDS ARE FOR

BET UP FRONT, Spring 2015.

UPTOWN party at HARLEM COVE. Fall 2015.

PUERTO RICO Xscape Puerto Rico 2018 festival (Red carpet/step and repeat). Memorial Day 2017.

SINGERS | 245

The 12x Grammy-nominated vocalist, Ledisi, at the premiere of "For Colored Girls" at Ziegfeld Theatre on October 25, 2010 in New York City.

Meli'sa Morgan performs for the post-set of the Harlem Art Crawl. April 2013.

Meli'sa Morgan was the featured performer at a Studio-54 inspired party that Musa Jackson Productions hired me to host. Also, in attendance was Kathy Sledge, First Ladies of Skyy and more. Labor Day 2015.

Backstage with Jennifer Hudson at her live Central Park performance as part of the "GMA Summer Concert Series" on "Good Morning America. June 2011.

Kimberly Nichole is a girl about town when she's in NYC. Here we are at an East Side NYC event that our girlfriend Sidra Smith put on for Sphatika Spa July 2015.

CeCe Peniston wrote her career-defining hit "Finally" while still in college. Once she pushed through a few background singing gigs, she had a short period of dance chart dominance starting with that gem before graduation. Then "We Got A Love Thang" and "Keep On Walkin." Her second project took on more of an urban R&B feel including "I'm In The Mood" and the quiet storm ballad "Inside That I Cried."

CeCe Peniston attends, The Face That Changed It All, Gala at Museum of the City of New York on September 9, 2015, in New York City.

Yolanda Adams, the super successful gospel singer who has sold more than 8 million records globally. hosting a Disney Dreamers Academy event in Philadelphia, PA at the National Association of Black Journalists convention.

CeCe Winans is the eighth Winans sibling. Born Priscilla in Detroit, she and her siblings say they came out of the womb singing in church. She and BeBe had a special chemistry, attracting the attention of the PTL club which recorded the duo's first album, **Lord Lift Us Up**, released on PTL in 1984, while they were PTL singers. Five major successful albums would follow. The biggest one being 1991's **Different Lifestyles**. Two of its singles, "Addictive Love" and the Staple Singers cover "I'll Take You There" featuring Mavis Staples crossed over and existed for weeks on the secular charts as well as the religious music charts. As they each went their own ways creatively, CeCe has continued an impressive ride of Grammy-award-winning album releases, now splitting her time co-pastoring a church in Nashville with her husband Alvin.

San Diego at the NABJ Gospel Brunch with CeCe Winans, featured performer for the annual event. July 2010.

Mary Mary is a duo comprised of sisters Erica and Tina Atkins. Inglewood, California is their home. Their parents were gospel singers and the children followed suit. Once Mary Mary signed as a recording act to Columbia/C2 Records and released the classic single "Shackles, Praise You," they got their first acquaintance with the top of the charts. And in this instance, they crossed over. This Christian song was being played in the club just like much of the material in their almost 20-year repertoire. They now perform solo and have received additional nods from the industry for those projects.

At Brooklyn's Two Steps Down Restaurant for the release party of Mary Mary's CD, The Sound.

May 2015. Elle Varner came by Arise Entertainment 360 on one of the days that I was hosting. She serenaded us as well.

Cheryl Pepsii Riley is best known for her 1988 ballad "Thanks for My Child." She's also starred in Tyler Perry's stage plays, Madea's Class Reunion and Why Did I Get Married?

September 2010. With Cheryl Pepsii Riley for lunch in Harlem at Mobay Uptown.

Grammy-nominated R&B and soul singer Syleena Johnson is known for her Chapter series of studio albums. She got international fame as the featured vocalist on Kanye West's "All Falls Down." She starred in the reality series **R&B Diva** and currently is a co-host for **Sister Circle** Live!

At 'R&B Divas' private viewing at Corner Social.

Mary Wilson is one of the original Supremes – still known as the biggest girl group of their time. Mary Wilson continued the function as a Supreme for eight years after Diana Ross left the group in 1970. In 1979, Mary went solo and has continued to perform the Supremes songs and more. Her legend shines as brightly as Miss Ross when the name Supremes comes up. Mary is also a New York Times best-selling author for her memoir on her Motown days, **Dreamgirl: My Life as a Supreme** and **Supreme Faith: My Life After the Supremes**.

Mary Wilson Labor Day 2017 at the Riverfront Jazz Festival where she did a set with Freda Payne and Eloise Laws.

Mary Wilson at the African American Museum in Philadelphia September 2012 for a one-on-one chat time with Miss Ross' fellow Original Supreme, the FABULOUS Mary Wilson whose exhibition, **Come See About Me: The Mary Wilson Supremes Collection** ran at the African American Museum in Philadelphia.

SINGERS | 253

Kelly Rowland is a member of the top-selling American R&B girl group Destiny's Child. Her record sales are at 50 million and she has won multiple Grammy Awards with the group.

Kelly Rowland in 2011 at a Christmas party in Atlanta.

Kelly Rowland at the Hudson Hotel in NYC for a listening party moderated by Gayle King. May, 2010.

Rozonda "Chilli" Thomas and I have been associates since her pre-TLC college days at Georgia Southern. She went on to sing on some of the biggest hits of the '90s and 2000s. TLC would eventually sell 45 million albums worldwide. Their sophomore album, **CrazySexyCool,** and the next album, **FanMail**, were Grammy winners. Four singles went to No. 1, including "No Scrubs" and "Waterfalls."

El Debarge has been a buddy for some years through his cousins Shelly & Sherry. Slate in New York City. December 2010. El Debarge listening party.

In 2012, Claudette Robinson was inducted into the Rock and Roll Hall of Fame with the rest of the original Miracles including Bobby Rogers, her cousin, as well as Pete Moore, Ronald White, Marv Tarplin, and her former husband, Miracles lead singer, Smokey Robinson.

I'm standing between Diana Ross & Berry Gordy's daughter, Rhonda Ross and Claudette Robinson.

Martha Reeves and the Vandellas are in the Rock & Roll Hall of Fame. This is no surprise given their Motown hits "Dancing in the Street" and "Heat Wave." Their handful of hits will play in the soundtrack of our lives forever.

Martha Reeves at Aretha Franklin's birthday party in Detroit. March 2008.

256 | THAT'S WHAT FRIENDS ARE FOR

Hendryx is best known as one of the original members of the iconic space-age girl group, Labelle. Nona has transformed throughout her career from a founding member of The Bluebelles to a solo artist, songwriter and producer and now a visual artist.

April 2013. With Nona Hendryx on the Opening Night of Motown the Musical.

December 2008. After the legendary Labelle gave a reunion concert at the historic Apollo Theater, we all gathered at a nearby Harlem brownstone for after set featuring Labelle's soprano Sarah Dash and Labelle's music director John Stanley. One of my favorite writers David Nathan, "Soulful Divas," flew in from the UK for this momentous event.

Mel B is known as Scary Spice. The Spice Girls have sold over 80 million records globally. They are the best-selling girl group in the world. Their single "Wannabe" hit no.1 in 37 countries. She continues to work as a TV personality on **America's Got Talent**.

I interviewed Mel B for recurring client on **Oprah, Where Are They Now**? at the SOHO Grand. March 2013, but sometimes I simply bump into her on the street.

Michelle Williams, who became a member of Destiny's Child, on her opening night on Broadway in Chicago. February 2011.

I worked with Michelle Williams for the NBC Universal, The More You Know, PSA campaign for 2015-16. I was the executive producer, and she was promoting her Oxygen **Fix My Choir** show with Deitrick Haddon. October 2014.

April 2014. Having lunch at Tijuana Garage in Atlanta with Destiny's Child original Latavia Roberson.

Normani is the one African American member of Fifth Harmony, a girl group that was put together on the reality singing competition **X Factor**. As a group, they've gone on to major success. Normani is beginning to step out on her own to do more modeling, TV personality work and solo music.

In March 2014, I sat in a photo shoot with Fifth Harmony that was doubling as a b-roll shoot for **The Keke Palmer Show**.

chapter 13
The Creatives

There's a famous black-and-white picture of Lorraine Hansberry, the black playwright who wrote *A Raisin in the Sun*, dancing with James Baldwin at what appears to be a '60s house party. Like me, Baldwin, a gay black man, loved intelligent black women. In addition to Hansberry, one of his best friends was the phenomenal black poet and memoirist Maya Angelou.

In fact, it was James Baldwin who, by arranging a dinner with Random House editor Robert Loomis, challenged Maya Angelou to write her first memoir, *I Know Why the Caged Bird Sings*, which was published the year I was born. This book was required reading for Advanced Placement English at my elementary school, and I identified with Angelou's coming-of-age tale tracing the emotional and transcendent journey of a little girl who survived rape and racism to find her voice as a self-assured young woman by the age of sixteen, showing incredible grace despite the oppression and cruelty of her humble beginnings in Stamps, Arkansas. Many books, a poem for Bill Clinton's inauguration, and hundreds of *Oprah Winfrey Show* episodes later, Angelou is an international treasure who inspires the creativity in me and so many others.

James Baldwin argued in his 1976 book-length essay, *The Devil Finds Work*, that no black actors at the time, no matter how famous they were, ever fully expressed their talents on screen, constrained by a racist industry that limited their choices. What would he have said at the premiere of the 2016 film *I Am Not Your Negro*? This small, artistic documentary was directed by a black man, Raoul Peck, and based on Baldwin's unfinished manuscript, "Remember This House." Narrated by black actor Samuel L. Jackson and nominated at the 89th Annual Academy Awards ceremony for Best Documentary Feature, the film explores Baldwin's personal observations of American history, particularly his reminiscences of civil rights leaders Medgar Evers, Malcolm X, and Martin Luther King, Jr. Were he alive, Baldwin might very well have said that the repression of black creativity is no longer the norm in the film industry, then proudly pointed out that this is largely due to black women like Shonda Rhimes and a couple of other ladies I've gotten to know personally, including multimedia moguls Mara Brock Akil and Ava DuVernay, each of whom have exploded onto the small-screen and feature-film scenes.

Showrunners haven't typically been black females, but Shonda Rhimes broke through that glass ceiling, heading a handful of network hits that put ABC in good standing with advertisers. The bonanza started with the medical drama *Grey's Anatomy* and its spinoff, *Private Practice*, as well as the political thriller *Scandal*, starring black actress Kerry Washington, and another caper, *How to Get Away with Murder*, also starring a black actress, Viola Davis. TIME *Magazine* named Rhimes one of its 100 People Who Help Shape the World, and in 2015 she published a memoir, *Year of Yes: How to Dance It Out, Stand in the Sun, and Be Your Own Person*. In addition to being one of primetime's most reliable hit makers in the more than twelve years since her first series, Rhimes now has a lucrative network deal with online-streaming service Netflix. Creatives take risks, and Rhimes' inspirational example has a whole nation of diverse people cheering her on.

Mara Brock Akil began her career in 1994, writing for the critically acclaimed but short-lived Fox series *South Central*. In 1999, she served as a supervising producer and writer for *The Jamie Foxx Show* after writing for four seasons of *Moesha*. I met her and her husband, black director and producer Salim Akil, in 2000, when she and Kelsey Grammer were executive producing a UPN series she had created,

Girlfriends, starring black actress Tracee Ellis Ross, which is one of my favorites. I've been asking her to make a *Girlfriends* reunion ever since UPN canceled the show without a finale even though it had a loyal following for eight seasons. She also created and executive produced the *Girlfriends* spinoff series, *The Game*, starring Tia Mowry, another black actress, which after a short run on UPN was picked up by BET and given a handful of new seasons that were more popular than the initial ones. In 2009, she was a consulting producer and writer for *Cougar Town*, a sitcom on ABC. As the creator of BET's *Being Mary Jane*, which premiered in 2013 and has now wrapped up as a two-hour movie, her profile has attracted business with iconic brands like Warner Brothers and the Oprah Winfrey Network.

I met Ava DuVernay when her public relations firm, The DuVernay Agency, was heading the campaign to launch the movie *Dreamgirls* in 2006. Even though we worked closely together at the time, little did I know that she had other films on her mind. After some training in film school, DuVernay made her directorial debut in 2008 with the documentary *This Is the Life*, a history of L.A.'s Good Life Cafe art movement, having decided to begin with documentaries so she could learn the trade on a smaller budget than with feature films. By 2011, she debuted her first feature film, *I Will Follow*, to critical acclaim and industry praise. This drama, starring black actress Salli Richardson-Whitfield, was made in fourteen days at a cost of only $50,000. Roger Ebert called it "one of the best films I've seen about coming to terms with the death of a loved one." DuVernay's next feature, *Middle of Nowhere*, made her the first black woman to win the Best Director Award at the 2012 Sundance Film Festival. Her notoriety and good work continued to grow in 2014 when the film *Selma*, based on the 1965 voting rights marches from Selma to Montgomery led by Martin Luther King, Jr., Hosea Williams, James Bevel, John Lewis, and others, brought DuVernay the first Golden Globe Award nomination for a black female director. In 2017, she was nominated again as the director of the documentary *13th*. But DuVernay didn't rest on her laurels: her next film, *A Wrinkle in Time*, reportedly has a budget exceeding $100 million.

African-American women have always been creatives. From the cornmeal and intestines they turned into delicacies to the fabric scraps they turned into artistic blankets, they've created beauty out of unimaginable hardship. Through the creative leadership of women like these, a new level of diversity in films has arisen that is distinct from past spurts of progress.

British director Amma Asante recently asked if a black woman was "even 'allowed' to be named an 'auteur'." Of course black women can excel in the arts, but will they be given a chance to create a body of work worthy of study, reverence, and—dare we say—funding? In the wake of #OscarsSoWhite, black filmmakers seem to be finally getting the attention, budgets, and awards they are due. The 2017 Oscars reflected well the growing diversity of Hollywood: black actor Mahershala Ali and Viola Davis respectively took home the awards for Best Supporting Actor and Best Supporting Actress, and I was certainly proud to see the film *Moonlight*, based on black playwright Tarell Alvin McCraney's unpublished semi-autobiographical play, "In Moonlight, Black Boys Look Blue," which explores the struggles of LGBTQ existence in the black community through the eyes of a young Miami boy who grows up enduring much abuse and shame about his sexuality, win for Best Adaptive Screenplay and Best Picture. We have also entered a golden age of black television, accompanied by an embarrassment of riches from hit series such as *Atlanta, Insecure, Queen Sugar, Being Mary Jane, Black-ish, Scandal, How to Get Away with Murder, Empire,* and *Power.* What would James Baldwin have said about Ava DuVernay's television adaptation of black author Natalie Baszile's novel, *Queen Sugar*, especially since DuVernay has not only served as its executive producer, showrunner, co-writer, and occasional director but also hired all female directors for its first season on black female billionaire Oprah Winfrey's network? Black producers, writers, and directors should use this unprecedented opportunity to advance the interests of the black community by fully harnessing their creativity.

SCRAPBOOK

Janet Jackson hosted Tim Palen's 'For Colored Girls' Living Portraits opening-night reception at Lehmann Maupin Gallery in New York City on October 24, 2010. Also present was Ntozake Shange, who authored the poetic monologue For Colored Girls Who Have Considered Suicide/When the Rainbow Is Enuf, on which the exhibit was based.

I knew Mara Brock Akil's work before it was famous. She was a writer for the short-lived Fox series **South Central**, a supervising producer and writer for **The Jamie Foxx Show**, and a writer for four seasons of **Moesha**. But everything changed when she created and executive produced the UPN series **Girlfriends** in partnership with Kelsey Grammer, from which she spun off a show called **The Game** that went on to be a major success for BET, the network that also aired her next brainchild, **Being Mary Jane**. She and her husband, Salim Akil, co-creator of **The Game** and director of the films **Jumping the Broom** and **Sparkle**, have been making more TV magic, giving the CW its biggest debut in over two years: the DC Comics—based superhero series **Black Lightning**, for which Salim has served as showrunner. The couple's next project is **Love Is __** on the Oprah Winfrey Network.

It was great to attend the 16th Annual Urbanworld Film Festival, held in September 2012 at the AMC Loews 34th Street 14 theater in New York City, for the opening night of the BET Premiere Cinema film **Being Mary Jane** created and written by Mara Brock Akil. In attendance along with the Akils was the star of the film, Gabrielle Union, as well as her co-stars, Richard Brooks and Tika Sumpter, and the casting director, Tracy "Twinkie" Byrd.

Vy Higginsen was the first female advertising executive at **Ebony** magazine, then became a radio personality for outlets like WBLS and WWRL and even a television reporter on WNBC and The Metro Channel. In 1983, Higginsen co-wrote, co-produced, and narrated the musical **Mama, I Want to Sing!** that tells the story of her sister Doris Troy, which spun off stage sequels and was adapted into a movie. In 1998, Higginsen founded the Mama Foundation for the Arts, a nonprofit arm of her creative outlets, where many young people, including her daughter Knoelle, have been spotlighted. Since 2006, the foundation has also offered free gospel-music instruction to teenagers in a program called Gospel for Teens.

Vy Higginsen and I were invited to the April 2013 after-party at the Red Rooster for the premiere of the NAACP Image Award—winning documentary **Free Angela and All Political Prisoners** produced by my dear friend Sidra Smith and executive produced by Jada Pinkett Smith, Will Smith, and Jay-Z.

In 2006, I had the opportunity to a host a **Dreamgirls** sneak peak in Indianapolis featuring my interview with Jennifer Hudson, who has since won an Oscar and a Grammy for her role in the film. As arranged by then-publicist Ava DuVernay, DreamWorks brought clips fresh from the Cannes Film Festival with a little extra for the National Association of Black Journalists. Hudson performed three songs, two of them from the film, with just one mic and a piano in front of 200 excited journalists and her immediate family, who drove in from Chicago. Since meeting DuVernay at that event, I've witnessed firsthand her back-to-back hit film work, starting with the short film **Middle of Nowhere**, followed by the epic Martin Luther King, Jr. story **Selma** and the in-your-face documentary **13th**. Then DuVernay created and executive produced the hit series **Queen Sugar** for the Oprah Winfrey Network, and she has become the first black woman to direct a $100-million film, the new adaptation of the classic fantasy novel **A Wrinkle in Time**.

Director Ava DuVernay screened her short film **Middle of Nowhere** in Philadelphia at the National Association of Black Journalists convention in July 2011.

In October 2015, I attended a special New York City screening of **Selma** followed by a Q&A session with Ava DuVernay.

In February 2015, I interviewed Crystal McCrary with Sharon Carpenter on **Arise Entertainment 360**.

In July 2017, I hosted a screening of **Detroit** featuring a talkback session with Al Sharpton and author and film producer Crystal McCrary (**Little Ballers**).

At the engagement party of Shirley Madhere and Michael Weill at the New York Public Library, it was nice to see Crystal McCrary, as well as B Michael, who dressed Madhere in his "Advanced American Style" for the evening's dancing.

Gina Prince-Bythewood wrote and directed the widely acclaimed feature film **Love & Basketball**, which premiered at the 2000 Sundance Film Festival, where it received the Film Independent Spirit Award for Best First Feature. Prince-Bythewood also directed and produced HBO's Disappearing Acts in 2000. She earned her first feature-film producer credit in **Biker Boyz**, a 2003 film co-written and directed by her husband, Reggie Rock Bythewood. I interviewed her when she directed **The Secret Life of Bees** in 2008.

In June 2014, I interviewed Gina Prince-Bythewood at a press junket in New York City for her film **Beyond the Lights**.

Sheila E. started as a drummer and singer for the George Duke band in the mid-1970s. After leaving the group in 1983, Sheila E. began a successful solo career, starting with her critically acclaimed debut album, which included her career-making hit, "The Glamorous Life." Her additional hits are "The Belle of St. Mark," "Sister Fate," and "A Love Bizarre." Many call her the Queen of Percussion.

In October 2009, Sheila E. and I attended the Jackie Robinson Foundation's annual Jazz on the Grass at Oz and Lynne Scott's Sherman Oaks estate. James Pickens, Jr. of **Grey's Anatomy** fame is in the shot with us.

chapter 14
Journalists

In 2014, I was too excited to be back home in Savannah as a keynote speaker for the Savannah State University Media High program's closing ceremony and luncheon. In attendance was my favorite teacher Mrs. Linda Green, who taught me typing and other business courses, which to this day informs how quickly I churn out a script, email or social media post in my current life as an entertainment journalist. Mrs. Green was my buddy. In an era of dual cassette stereos and vinyl LPs, she asked me to do a mix tape of her favorite songs: Side A wasc Diana Ross and Side B was Dionne Warwick. On any given morning, she and I would recap a primetime moment or two from the night before, whether *The Cosby Show* or *Dynasty*.

As the adviser for the Ascendants, sort of a black student union, Mrs. Green freed all of us students to express our greatness and that of our many unsung foremothers and forefathers who didn't always have a spotlight to exclaim their stories. As my ambitions further took shape, Mrs. Green was personally key in ensuring I could accept an after-school job offer from Chief WTOC anchor Doug Weathers, on the heels of a career day visit that she organized, ensuring that I got to go to my first choice, a TV station. The gig that came on the heels of that visit was to be "teleprompter" for the 5p and 6p newscasts. In order to do it, Mrs. Green had to get further involved, giving me a ride to get my mom's car from her job around the corner, Kinder Care, so I could do the gig and be back for Mom by her day's wrap.

It's the only way my mom would let me do it. And so, it was. Lots has changed since 1988, but that day in 2014 when I saw my favorite teacher for the first time in some years, I was moved at how my gratitude for all that she taught me and did for me was right in the choke of my throat. And what was great is I got to say "thank you" again and in front of a room of high school journalists from Savannah. My dad was in the room as well.

It's my dad who says my ambitions were present from childhood. I always knew I wanted to pursue journalism, so I wrote, produced and presented on a student level since elementary school.

And through it all, I daydreamed no less about the women of color in the news business. They were my industry divas whose expertise shined in the direction of what I actually knew I wanted to do. What local, black anchors Teresa Minor, Malena Cunningham and Arthur Fennell presented to the local news audience in Savannah, I channeled, if just for a high school presentation. Whenever I looked at one of those Sunday public affairs programs, I liked the idea of packaging information for people to be able to do more to help their fellow man. I became a teen peer counselor because, early on, I wanted to be helpful and informative, similar to what I began to experience of my local TV talent,

Bryant Gumbel was a childhood idol who is best known for his fifteen years as co-host of NBC's *Today Show*, and I watched him every day from 6th grade until I was in my mid-20s. He was so articulate and handsome. He could handle the heavy-weight newsmakers and still give proper reverence and kiss up to the A-listers. When he needed to be snarky, he could channel it, and quickly. He was my kind of guy on *Today*.

It's at this same time that I got word from *Ebony* that there were two African Americans on ABC News that were available to be watched prominently. Founding member of the National Association of Black Journalists, Max Robinson became the first black man to anchor a nightly news broadcast. During this time, Max established a program for mentoring young black broadcast journalists. By the mid-80s, he'd left ABC News and retired. News that he had AIDS would rock the industry. By December 1988, he was dead. I have continued to speak Max's name as I continue to be an active member of NABJ. So many men of color who are journalists owe a great debt to him.

I got the chance to actually meet and eventually produce another NABJ member whose work is impressive, if unsung. When I was five years old, I was into the news. It wouldn't take much for me to recognize that this black woman, Carole Simpson, was on the air, first at NBC News where she became the first African-American woman to anchor a major network newscast. She was so pretty and delivered that news with the combined pacing of a kindergarten teacher and a drill sergeant. She has since established the Carole Simpson scholarship to encourage and help minority students overcome hurdles along their career path, which is offered annually to aspiring journalists.

Current journalists like Robin Roberts, *Access Hollywood*'s long-standing co-host Shaun Robinson and multi-Emmy-award-winning news correspondent, Mara Schiavocampo, have acknowledged Simpson as their forbearer and role model, an outspoken African-American female in a business that was long a boys' club. And they each have been an influence on me.

I don't know Robin Roberts personally but have been in her presence several times, once running into her on the set of *Good Morning America* while I was there in 2006 to interview then-host, Diane Sawyer for her recollections from the Oprah Legends Ball. I admired her since I was a freshman at Morehouse which aligned with her being hired by WAGA-TV as a sports anchor and reporter. Also, she was a radio host for hit R&B station V-103 and even then, I enjoyed Robin's down-home and polished personality. She left Atlanta to work for ESPN while I was still in college, but it was such a big deal that she landed that national gig which then led to her being a featured reporter for *Good Morning America*.

In 2013, Robin came out as a lesbian woman in a relationship with Amber Laign, a massage therapist and they have been together since 2005.

I always teach young folks to see who's doing it like you want to do it and try to mimic that route until you can make it your own. We've heard Oprah Winfrey say she acted as if she was Barbara Walters until she could find her own voice and personality. Though I have gotten to meet and know Shaun Robinson as a friend and colleague, I considered her trajectory one that I could follow until I found my way. She went to Diana Ross' high school in Detroit, Cass Technical High School. That detail alone was worth channeling. She is a Spelman College graduate. I am a Morehouse man and in 1999, I was enamored not just of the beauty and personality she presented as host of daily entertainment newsmagazine show *Access Hollywood*, I was moved at how helpful and nice she was. I was the chair of the NABJ Arts & Entertainment Task Force at the time. We always welcomed mentors and role models to power our programming with their testimonials and expertise. Since she started at *Access Hollywood*, she always said yes, and she would move everyone with her candor and support.

Shaun has become a mentor and friend, even ensuring that I was included in *Access Hollywood*'s coverage of Samuel L. Jackson's visit to our journalism convention in Las Vegas. Moreover, as I am living testimonial that it's important to lift the next generation even higher on the shoulders of our own mistakes, I still look to Shaun, a published author that spends extensive time working with girls on self-esteem. Her first book, *Exactly As I Am: Celebrated Women Share Candid Advice with Today's Girls on What it Takes to Believe in Yourself*, put together the collective wisdom of both superstar women and everyday teenagers.

Mara Schiavocampo was NABJ's Emerging Journalist of the Year when I met her in 2007. My girlfriend, Itika Oldwine, was an audience producer for *The Oprah Winfrey Show* and thought we'd hit it off. Moreover, she thought we should know each other. At the time, Mara was the first digital correspondent hire that NBC News brought into the fold, a history-making get that didn't require she be the first African American. She was just the first. Mara and I were also attuned to each-others ambitions, so we supported each other accordingly. She calls me her "internet husband" because often we are out and about, having fun and networking together. As Mara's work has now had her earn three Emmy awards and placement as a correspondent on *Today* and *Good Morning America*, she's always extended opportunities for me to get on the air with my pop culture analysis. During the era of Obama, she had me weigh in all the time, which informed other opportunities for me to not just be on-camera but presenting my preferred genre, entertainment.

From 2013-2015, I was a recurring guest co-host for New York City-based *Arise Entertainment 360*, a magazine show in which I presented hot topics alongside co-host Lola Ogunnaike. We also conducted interviews, demo and cooking segments and roundtables. Often, the same talent that Access Hollywood was interviewing, was coming to be interviewed by me including some of my favorites singers like Tamia and Faith, authors like Tavis Smiley and Alan Light, and actors like Antonio Fargas and Ben Vereen. From the pages of *O Magazine*, I sometimes got to interview friends of mine, like Miss Robbie and Tim Norman from *Welcome to Sweetie Pie's* and filmmaker Crystal McCrary, director of the documentary *Little Ballers*.

On and on, I could go on the examples of how this particular sorority of women lifts me up daily. Surely, I still diva worship them when their glam squad gets their look just right, their couture is tight, and they delivered that line with just the perfect dose of sass that might be worth rewinding. I cry with them, if they are leaving their station or network. There are many of them behind the scenes who, in some cases, were no less influential to me. Women like journalism education giant Ann Wead Kimbrough, who was my college advisor. While others told me, I needed to choose what I wanted to do, from medium to the actual job, Dr. Kimbrough led by example, letting me know that I could do anything I wanted, and at the same time, if I chose. While she was teaching a host of others and me, she was a regular financial contributor on WSB-TV, a business editor for *Atlanta Business Chronicle*, and eventually she would add media consulting, public relations and government communications to her resume. She always lands, and impressively, but she never stops helping others in big ways. She introduced me to her best buddy at the time, the late *Good Day Atlanta* Executive Producer Sidmel Estes-Sumpter who as she was making history as the first woman President of NABJ was also taking the hand of this recent Morehouse graduate to ensure the first steps of my career would give me longevity. When I was growing out of Atlanta, CNBC anchor Sheila Stainback came to the rescue and ensured I was relocated and hired to work for Geraldo's primetime show *Rivera Live* which was a move that got me to New York City. When I was ready to break away from the intensity of hard news, Paula Madison first came calling. She was the first African-American woman to be the news director for the #1 station in New York City, WNBC. She brought me on as a special projects producer which, a year later, opened the door for my fellow NABJ intern Candi Carter. Then in 1998, Candi was a producer for *The Oprah Winfrey Show*, making it possible for me to be a contract freelance field producer until the show's wrap, my main and most lucrative client to this day. And it would be Harlem's own Bevy Smith, who, as she has herself made the industry embrace her as a TV talent of note, made it possible for me to be hired as a regular pop culture analyst on TV One's *Life After*, a show that catches up with entertainers and newsmakers from the a noted period in their career, including Levar Burton, Sheree Whitfield, Jimmie Walker, Sheryl Lee Ralph, Maia Campbell, Clifton Davis and others.

Having lost my mom when I was 23 years old, I must say that I chose the right industry to have a host of surrogates to lead me on to my success and the modicum of joy I'm able to muster without Mom. In lieu, I have my industry moms and sister friends who get me through.

SCRAPBOOK

Sharon Carpenter is a British import that the American airwaves love. Her award-winning work ranges from hosting to producing. Her media outlets include CBS, BET, VH1, BBC America, Arise, and Sean "Diddy" Combs' REVOLT TV. She is the co-founder of Wiretapped, an entertainment news site and live video platform. And she's even had a cameo on Fox prime-time hit Empire, playing a cool, calm, and collected journalist Co-Hosting alongside Sharon Carpenter for Arise Entertainment 360, Spring 2015.

Lola Ogunnaike is currently Host of **EW: The Show**, a Pen original weekly series. She and I worked alongside each other or a few years starting in 2013 when she would bring me in to guest host alongside her on **Arise Entertainment 360**. Before TV, Lola was a reporter for The New York Times as well as a writer for **Vibe** magazine, contributing to the monthly music features and cover stories. Rolling Stone, New York, Glamour, Details (magazine), Nylon, the New York Observer and V Magazine call on Lola for her writing talents. Her entertainment expertise and insights are sought globally.

Tamron Hall is still working on her talk show that she will host. She left being co-host of **Today's Take**, the third hour of Today, to pursue new opportunities.

I booked Tamron Hall to moderate the post-screening Q&A of **The Help** for the arts & entertainment journalists in attendance at a July 2011 event. She's always a great host or presenter for a live event.

Was great to arrange for Miss Jessie's CEO Miko Branch to be honored by the Black Women's Health Initiative at the Congressional Black Caucus in Washington DC. September 2017. Tamron Hall was also honored.

Bevy Smith has been a true NYC industry friend—supporting my projects and inviting me to her projects—including her Dinner with Bevy that introduced me to the exec that made one of my immediate goals come true: to be a TV ONE on-cam pop culture analyst for one of its docu-strips LIFE AFTER.

in All-Star Karaoke since the beginning and always encourages that part of me. She loves my, "Can't Let Go" by Mariah Carey and "This Woman's Work" Maxwell. In this pic, Bevy is interrupting my news read prep to ready for the segment in which I'm going to interview she and her, at the time, co-stars from Fashion Queens, Miss Lawrence and Derek J.

Mara Schiavocampo is a multi-Emmy-award-winning network journalist. She is also a published author for her memoir **Thinspired: How I lost 90 Pounds**. Her network career started in 2007 when she began serving NBC News as a digital correspondent and anchor of the show, **Early Today**. And she manages it all with her husband Tommie, daughter Nina and son Cruz.

I was Mara Schiavocampo's date at Black Girls Rock at NJPAC in Newark, March 2015. She presented. We were seated up front and captured often throughout the production.

Cheryl Washington has over twenty years of journalism experiences in media outlets including CNN, WABC-TV, WCBS-TV, WNBC-TV, CNN, and FOX 5.

In Newark, NJ on Fall 2011, I was happy to meet Cheryl Washington who was in attendance at Miss Robbie Montgomery and her son **Tim's Welcome to Sweetie Pie's** screening.

Shaun Robinson has been my NABJ sister friend for many years from her local markets, like Milwaukee and Detroit. Shaun hosted Access Hollywood, the daily entertainment newsmagazine show from 1999 to 2015. She was also the host of **TV One Access**, a show on the TV One network produced by Access.

Shaun Robinson and I at the NABJ Convention in Las Vegas, July 2007.

Monica Pearson is the Queen of Atlanta news. She joined WSB-TV in 1975 as Atlanta's first woman and first minority to anchor the daily 6 p.m. news. She also has anchored the 4, 5 and 11 p.m. news during her career, debuting the 4 and 5. And 37 years later, she called it a career at WBS while she continues to do TV and radio in the marketplace. Monica is a true legend.

I say it all the time, but still don't mind exclaiming that among my highlights, I was Monica Pearson's intern at WSB-TV. We do grown folks business these days including her support of my Brand Ambassador work with Miss Jessie's, inviting Miss Jessie's CEO Miko Branch to be a special, three-hour guest on her Sunday KISS 104.1 show, a kick-off for Black History Month 2017.

As Monica Pearson receives a Lifetime Achievement Award at NABJ in New Orleans 2012, her favorite interns congratulate her, my girlfriend Audrey who was a Senior at CAU (now a Senior exec at CNN) and me.

While a Senior at Morehouse College, I interned for legendary anchor Monica Pearson. Fast forward to 2011, I was on the producing team that activated the surprise for the Oprah Farewell Spectacular: 475 Morehouse scholars for whom Oprah was a benefactor came through the United Center like "candles" in the dark, making for one of Oprah's "ugly cry" moments.

Paula Williams Madison is a former NBC Universal executive and is now CEO of a family investment group based in Chicago. She retired from NBC after more than 35 years in the news media. Having founded Williams Holdings, a real estate investment firm, with her brothers, she subsequently bought a majority share of The Africa Channel and the Los Angeles Sparks. Madison was named one of the "75 Most Powerful African Americans in Corporate America" by Black Enterprise Magazine in 2005 and in 2014 as one of the Outstanding 50 Asian Americans in Business. She is of African and Hakka descent. In 2015 she wrote the book Finding Samuel Lowe: China, Jamaica, Harlem about her grandfather's life and travels and her own visit to Guangdong.

Paula Madison is one of my (NABJ) National Association of Black Journalists MENTORS! At a time in my career when I needed to "attract" skill-set work in entertainment and pop culture, she, at the helm of News 4 New York quickly and deliberately stepped in and up and presented me a handful of opportunities to shine via the local news division's special projects unit. The year was 1997 and to that moment, I became a "working" full-time, independent producer, personality, and writer. And the melody lingers on.

Summer 2012 with Paula Madison in New Orleans at the National Association of Black Journalists' Convention.

chapter 15
Women of Hip Hop

While the diva in me always adored R&B, hip-hop was the music of my generation. It rose up around me. Before we even knew what to call it, we knew it was something different and special, and women were a big reason why.

As my lens goes, I have to thank Diana Ross first. Sure, she's from the Brewster Projects in Detroit, Michigan. By the time I knew her, she was as important to me as the Queen of England to the Brits. And at five years old when I saw *Mahogany* introduce, what I would find out was one of the five pillars of hip hop, graffiti. Tracy Chambers is a sassy industrious young woman living in the projects of Chicago who dreams of becoming a fashion designer. As the aspiring designer wrapped up her night school sketch class, she commutes home. Seated on the subway she continues to sketch a pleated gown with dolman sleeves. As she sees a kid spraying graffiti on the walls of the subway, she's inspired to bring that vibrant touch to her design. As I grew older and began to hear how everything new and exciting started on the "streets," that transitional moment the film underscored that so vividly for me, leading to other hip-hop elements like rapping, DJing, breakdancing and beatboxing.

I lived in Savannah at the time I had first heard the Sugarhill Gang, an American hip-hop group known mostly for their 1979 hit "Rapper's Delight."

I loved the beat and as a singer, I considered it reductive and a trend as it began to best songs that I held dear for a more traditional arrangement and composition. But as a child, if there's a good beat, we just dance.

As iconography goes, and since I love the ladies, I did pay attention when female hip-hoppers popped up. The sequence was the first female old school hip-hop trio signed to the Sugar Hill label in 1979. The group consisted of Cheryl Cook (Cheryl the Pearl), Gwendolyn Chisolm (Blondie) and lead singer/rapper Angie Brown Stone (Angie B.). Columbia, South Carolina was home for this group of high-school cheerleaders. 1le solo rapper to win a Grammy for her Best Rap Single for 1993's "Ruffneck." She is thus, another of these First Ladies of Hip Hop. They managed to rise above the complications of misogyny, adversity, economic hardship, incarceration, sexual abuse/objectification and violence. That which many women in the world of hip-hop endured.

Diana didn't stop trying to get in on the fun of hip hop as she'd so successfully crossed over into many genres over her career, from Motown to the American Songbook to jazz to disco to country to pop. In 1989, she released the Nile-Rodgers-produced, "Workin' Overtime," her first Motown album since the bestselling studio album *Diana* from 1980 after Diana left the label for a then-record breaking $20 million deal with RCA. At this time, Motown founder Berry Gordy Jr. sold the label to MCA Records but arranged a deal that gave Diana a piece of Motown plus her recording contract if she returned. For Diana's Motown comeback, she brought her golden oldie audience some new jack swing, hip-hop and house music. "I stayed off work for about a year. I was having my babies and during that time I spent a lot of time watching BET on television, the kids doing the hip-hop and so on and, you know, I'm a risk taker."

The risk didn't calculate into amazing sales, but the title track did reach No. 3 on the Billboard R&B singles chart, in some part due to an urban, edgy Rose-Perez-choreographed video that features Diana decked out in a black leather biker jacket, a white tank top, ripped acid-wash jeans and boots! She's in the club doing all the dances of the day, including the running man.

Miss Ross is truly one of the queens of hip-hop. One of MC Lyte's biggest hits sampled Miss Ross' #1 hit, "Upside Down." "Cold Rock a Party" is the lead single released from Lyte's fifth studio album, *Bad as I Wanna B*. "My mom, she played Al Green. She played Barry White and Diana Ross and Donna Summer," the rapper said in a 2006 statement. "These are the people that gave me the strength to speak about what I love to speak about. Not only that but not be afraid to talk about who I am and what I want. Just be real on record."

Puff Daddy used the "real Diana Ross" on The Notorious B.I.G.'s second single from his posthumously-released album, *Life After Death*, "Mo Money Mo Problems." "I'm Coming Out!" is heard right off the top of the track, which leads you to think it might be the original Diana recorded with Nile Rodgers and Bernard Edwards. At closer inspection, my ears hear a sample of the low-pitched version of the Diana Ross song including backing vocals which repeat the title of that song. The new refrain was in fact sung by Kelly Price. Based on airplay and chart success the song is considered one of the most popular singles in hip-hop history. The single topped the Billboard Hot 100 for two weeks in 1997, replacing "I'll Be Missing You" from the chart which was Puff Daddy's tribute to Biggie's death.

Miss Ross has kept her boss' eye on the industry as well. When Diana came out to present the Best Hip-Hop Video with Lil Kim and Mary J. Blige at the MTV Music Awards, she was taken aback by her rapping co-presenter's much-buzzed-about-ensemble, a jumpsuit that dipped below her left breast, allowing it to roam free except for a pastie atop her nipple. Miss Ross' maternal finger went right to Kim's cleavage as if to say, "What are you not wearing girl?"

Eight years later, Diana was feted by the BET Awards with a Lifetime Achievement Award. She received a multi-song tribute from Erykah Badu, Chaka Khan and Stevie Wonder. Her five children including singer Rhonda Ross and actors Tracee Ellis Ross and Evan Ross, actually presented the prize after saying some lovely words to a packed house of hip-hop giants from back in the day through to 2007. Perhaps Lil' Kim was on her mind.

"I have tried to keep the standards high," she said. "We do not have to say the F-word, we do not have to pump and grind, we do not have to do some of these things to have longevity in our career."

The Boss obviously knows what she's talking about. President Obama agreed when he presented her America's highest civilian honors, the Medal of Freedom. "Today, from the hip-hop that samples her to the young singers who've been inspired by her, to the audiences that still cannot get enough of her, Diana Ross's influence is inescapable as ever."

That's why she continues to preach, "If you see something, say something." Jay-Z was 47 years old when he admitted his wrongdoings on his latest Grammy-nominated set *4:44*. Jay-Z offers a great example of how power and enablement go hand in hand. On the brutally honest single "4:44," he speaks openly about his lack of maturity in a relationship and the ensuing infidelity to that behavior. Still, he is an imperfect role model on how gentlemen can arch through their issues to be solid. It seems like only yesterday that Jay Z was spouting misogynistic lyrics in his classic "Big Pimpin'" such as "You know I, thug em', fuck em', love em', leave em', cause' I don't fuckin' need 'em."

Rick Ross once went on air and said he'd never sign a female rapper because he'd have to get involved with her sexually, so he'd rather pass instead. Buzzfeed's investigative piece on the R. Kelly sex cult and its rapid trivialization all happened within the last year. Do you remember the video that surfaced of VLONE's A$AP Bari pulling a naked girl out of bed in a room with two other men and forcing her into another room, saying she would have to have sex with him? Days later, Bari and A$AP Rocky were out chilling together at FYF.

Hip-hop has always had a serious problem with the female gender. Most of the time women are viewed solely as a visual accessory or sexual object. This is nothing new. Dr. Dre is reformed and redeemed inside of the cinematic retelling of his life "Straight Out of Compton," but there's no erasing his well-documented assault on Dee Barnes. The list of incidents in recent memory goes on. These include Famous Dex, Ian Connor, Kodak Black and let's not forget

Chris Brown who managed to get off or get over in the court of public opinion, becoming a worldwide icon again thanks to people's short memories and attention span not to mention their willingness to overlook violence against women.

While some listeners, DJs and publications have removed these artists from daily rotation, most have not. There seems to be a hatred for women inside their vibration, but we still lift them up. While criticism of the artists is heard, many of those guilty of feeding this beast still have huge followings, regardless of what they do. Famous Dex did lose his spot on the XXL Freshman list and Rick Ross did lose his Reebok deal due to another scandal over lyrics about slipping molly into an unwitting girl's drink.

On that anecdote alone, hip-hop is obviously not the only culprit that is complicit in this trend of disrespecting women. Hopefully, the First Ladies of Hip Hop that I admire will raise their voices and be that difference. Ladies First, right Latifah? Stop it with the acts of sexual harassment, domestic violence and rape.

Out of every 1000 rapes, it's estimated that only 310 are reported. If we've been shown over and over again that there is no recourse for these actions, pressing charges just seems like more risk. Especially when the perpetrators are as powerful as these artists are. It seems as though rappers are held to no standard because of their status.

For hip-hop to continue growing, we must be the better example. Listening to any of the above-mentioned artists does not make somebody a bad person. Maybe some of the artists will eventually grow and evolve into better people. Hey, anything is possible. But until that happens, we can't feed into the already counterproductive culture that exists within our broader society. Hip-hop is a beautiful thing with an electric history and global influence. However, its issues must be faced and addressed by the First Ladies of Hip Hop. You'll win some and you'll lose some but must all say something.

SCRAPBOOK

Everybody loves the Queen! Famed musician and actress Queen Latifah's debut album, **All Hail to the Queen** was a record-breaking, million sellers and the single "U.N.I.T.Y." got her first Grammy Award. After a successful rapping career, she is a full-fledged actress earning her first Oscar nomination for her performance in the 2002 blockbuster musical Chicago, and an Emmy nod for her portrayal of blues singer Bessie Smith in the 2015 HBO film **Bessie**.

Queen Latifah at the Steel Magnolias premiere at The Paris Theatre, September 2012.

After starting her career as a backup singer on Uptown Records in 1989, the two-time Oscar nominee and multi-Grammy-winner Mary J. Blige released her first album, the now-iconic **What's the 411**, in 1992. She's released 13 studio albums since and made over 150 guest appearances on other albums and soundtracks. She reigns as the Queen of Hip Hop Soul.

I got to celebrate with Mary J. Blige at the release party for her new CD, **Growing Pains**. The festive set was held in the posh Soho Grand Hotel Penthouse Loft in December 2007.

Like many singers, Faith Evans started singing in the church. She won a full scholarship in high school to attend Fordham University, but she dropped out after a year to go directly for her singing pursuits. At 19, she met producer Sean "Diddy" Combs who eventually signed Faith to Bad Boy. She co-wrote and sang background vocals for Mary J. Blige's **My Life** CD. She first met rapper Notorious B.I.G. at a photo shoot in 1994. They married ten days after that meeting in August 1994. Her debut album, **Faith**, was a hit including singles "Soon as I Get Home," "You Used to Love Me" and "Ain't Nobody." Faith and Biggie had a son CJ, but eventually they split up. On March 8, 1997, Biggie was murdered near a Soul Train Music Awards party in Los Angeles, a party that Evans herself also had attended earlier in the night. Over the years, Faith has moved on but not without her with ups and downs, both personal and professional. But she's stayed true and loyal to her family, herself and Biggie's legacy.

Tiny is best known as a member of the American multi-platinum R&B vocal group Xscape. Her marriage with rapper T.I. Cottle is an industry in its own—best underscored by their hit VH1 show **T.I. and TINY: The Family Hustle**. Tiny and former Xscape member Kandi Burruss received a Grammy Award for writing TLC hit, "No Scrubs." Cottle acquired the nickname "Tiny" due to her small stature of 4'11." Tiny starred in **Tiny & Toya**. The original Xscape got back together for a super successful Winter 2017 tour. Now, the group navigates as a trio minus Kandi Burruss and they have new music and tour dates scheduled.

Kandi Burruss met the young girls who would become her Xscape group members at Tri-Cities High School in East Point, Georgia. She, LaTocha

Scott, Tamika Scott and finally Tameka "Tiny" Cottle found their way to BET's "Teen Summit," singing a Capella version of En Vogue's, "Hold On" with Tamika on the human beat box for percussion. Jermaine Dupris's So-So Def Recordings soon signed them and their debut album **Hummin' Comin' at 'Cha** was released in October 1993. It was a smash hit as were the two follow ups, "Off the Hook" in 1995 and "Traces of My Lipstick" in 1998. All three albums were certified platinum and spawned. Kandi had a little solo success as well with her debut album, **Hey Kandi** in 2000. By 2009, when she was starring on **The Real Housewives of Atlanta** on Bravo, she released an EP entitled **Fly Above** in 2009. She released another studio album, **Kandi Koated** in 2010. Her songwriting career is Grammy-award-winning as she has also enjoyed a prolific career of co-writing hits such as "No Scrubs" for TLC, "Bills, Bills, Bills" for Destiny's Child and "There You Go" for P!nk. Her reality success garnered her spin-off series, **The Kandi Factory** in 2012, **Kandi's Wedding** in 2014 and **Kandi's Ski Trip** in 2015. She made her Broadway debut in a special limited engagement as Matron 'Mama' Morton in Chicago.

Kandi at her Summer 2009 performance for Real Housewives of Atlanta. It took place at Tongue and Groove, coincidentally the location of my 1995 going-away party from Atlanta.

I met both Salt & Pepa at a book party Pepa had in 2008 or so.

Got to pose with Pepa at her VH1 viewing party in NYC Spring 2010.

chapter 16
All-Star Karaoke

As readers know by now, I come from a family of singers. Mom sang on the Mahalia Jackson level in her Savannah church since childhood. Dad sang four-part-harmony gospel when he was a teen. Think Frankie Lymon & the Teenagers on "Why Do Fools Fall in Love?" But for Jesus.

And I sang all the time too. The Riley kids, at least my brother Herman and me, inherited the singing gene. From early on, I had the cute, pre-op Michael Jackson swag going. So, there was always a song or a dance to do for mom and dad's friends when they came over to our house at Moody Air Force Base in Valdosta, GA.

I'm not sure who heard that I could sing first because I don't have a recollection of a home without someone singing in it. I do remember not being shy to deliver the goods. Though I was into the divas from early on, like Diana Ross, Dionne Warwick, Aretha Franklin and Roberta Flack, my cute, Michael Jackson swag let me get away with singing on "high." Though my brother and I could find dissonance about any subject, we provided just enough harmony and edge, the likes of Michael and Jermaine Jackson to offer some good chemistry for our audiences, usually of the neighborhood kind.

Growing up, I always got a kick out of seeing that dynamic on television when, in my favorite sitcoms, the actors would feature their singing talents in special episodes. Early on with *Good Times*, I remember when characters Florida and Thelma Evans along with neighbor

Wilona Woods decided to perform The Supremes "Stop! In the Name of Love" for a rent party to save a tenant. Esther Rolle, Bernadette Stanis and Ja'Net Dubois each got a verse, hence a chance to be Diana. A few years later on *Good Times*, Willona's adopted daughter Penny would be cast as none other than Janet Jackson. When Janet and Ralph Carter, as Michael Evans, sang together like when they channeled their inner-Sonny & Cher on the first episode in which Janet's character was introduced or the last season when they performed Billy Davis Jr. & Marilyn McCoo's *You Don't Have to Be A Star To Be in My Show*, I just loved those moments. The rush of seeing them stretch their creativity inside a situation. Their performances weren't always perfect, but they were inspired and had a film of energy on them. These shows air all the time, now on different cable networks. During that time, I had to be in front of the TV for the repeat and, since before VCRs, anytime the *TV Guide* told me it was playing in syndication. In the mid-70s, I really got a head rush when I found out that Ja'Net Dubois, Willona from *Good Times*, actually wrote and sang the theme song from *The Jeffersons* famously known as "Movin' On Up." As a four or five-year-old, I can remember feeling like the woman's singing voice was similar to a speaking voice I knew, but I couldn't quite place. Certainly, I stumbled into the information on a loaner from the library.

In 2009, I attended Judge Mablean Ephraim's Father's Day Event in Los Angeles. Ja'Net Dubois was in attendance. I let her know, in no uncertain terms, that she was an inspiration. She received my genuine love for her and the character of Wilona who, through the television screen, was such a friend in my head. I check in with her from time to time on TV One when the show airs on marathon.

Remember the infamous Bubbling Brown Sugar family that sang that show tune, then the little sister sang "God Bless the Child" on *What's Happening?* Ernest Thomas' Raj and Danielle Spencer's Dee were siblings and wanted to get this cute family booked on *The Gong Show*, a 1970s variety program hosted by Chuck Barris and featuring three judges who, if they didn't like the respective talent on the lineup, would get up and gong. One major success story from *The Gong Show* is one of my favorite singers Cheryl Lynn, who in 1976, got a perfect score and won that week for her moving rendition of Joe Cocker's, "You Are So Beautiful."

Audrey Givens was a sister in the group and I had the chance to meet her last year at a party I was hosting. And you would have thought I was meeting one of my divas because I appreciated how this little girl made me feel. And the curiosity that I have as a journalist would sometimes have me wondering where those kids are. Happy to say that Audrey, in 2014, was a contestant on BET's singing competition Sunday's Best and became a fan favorite. She's still singing and making things happen in order to have a career in entertainment. Fast forwarding to adolescence and adulthood, I continued to enjoy the variety show or living room talent show performances, like when Nell Carter as Nell from *Gimme A Break* goes home to Alabama and breaks out in song with her sister who was played by Lynn Thigpen and her best friend Addy was played by Telma Hopkins. They do a full out 60s girl group medley, singing "Soldier Boy," "He's My Rebel," "Stop! In The Name Of Love," "Big Girls Don't Cry" and "Heatwave." From the first note and all of the choreography, made to look natural, to the last note, these moments made me feel so happy. And when I stumble into them or look them up on YouTube, they are little blues busters.

In the '90s, high among my influences on this frequency is Tichina Arnold who, inside the last decade, has become a buddy when she's in town. I first got into Tichina as one of the girl group members in Frank Oz's *Little Shop of Horrors* musical from 1986. She was 15 at the time. The world came to know her when she was cast as Tisha Campbell Martin's best girlfriend. From 1992 to 1997, Gina and Tichina's Pam were ride or die. And when they sang, it was either funny or moving, but always a moment. On one episode, Martin had Pam and Gina sing BeBe & CeCe Winans' "Hold Up The Light," a tune the gospel duo recorded with Whitney Houston. As Tisha and Tichina had often worked together, their blend was magical. But Tichina, in that same episode, took everybody to church with her, "I Know

Who Holds Tomorrow." It's one of those moment that would begin to have our friends and me ask, "Why doesn't Tichina Arnold record an album?"

As Tichina is a friend of some dear friends, Sidra Smith and Carl Nelson, they enroll me into their social mix whenever Tichina is in town. Or sometimes, she'll ask for me. Like Mara Brock Akil, who doesn't mind when I ask her a litany of questions about her shows, Tichina has always been gracious to let me ask her anything about any of her work, from *Little Shop of Horrors* to *Martin*. And in recent years, we've spoken intimately about her work on *Everybody Hates Chris* and some of her more recent projects like *Survivor's Remorse* and *Daytime Divas*.

Beyond my own professional singing moments, I'm happy to say Tichina has that "let's break out in song" appeal in real life, a frequency I can be on socially as well. It's different than the shows I prepare to do. It's an in the moment kind of thing. One time, while at our girlfriend Sidra's Harlem apartment, Tichina and I were talking about her role on *Happily Divorced* with Fran Drescher and how much she enjoyed working with her. She spoke of how Fran was a big promoter of Tichina singing on the show. They even brought Jennifer Holliday on for a sing-off moment with Tichina. On that same visit, Tichina told us she could sing in Russian, and she did.

When Ant came into the picture, he conceived All-Star Karaoke as an event that I could host, on the frequency of those great moments in TV that I love so much and those inspired moments he'd seen me generate. Ant had grown used to my hogging the spotlight by 2010 when we were first asked to host a night. It's grown to be an open-mic that the Harlem community can count on for good vocals. This is when I took ownership of my falsetto and began to sing all of my childhood favorites. One highlight we always incorporate is "The Boss" which features "The Boss" choir, anyone who will come up and support the vocals on that big Diana disco hit from 1979.

The beautiful thing is, we are now attracting a host of people to our night who happen to be the ones who inspired me on TV, like

Tichina. In October 2010, she joined us for All-Star Karaoke when we were hosting it at a hip restaurant called Native. Tichina was in town co-starring in *Love, Loss, and What I Wore* at The Westside Theater, but told me she would come by our Thursday night event once she came down after the performance and could get changed. We kept the place open later for her as she wanted to eat as well. When Tichina walked in, I was in another nook of the small restaurant singing Mariah Carey's, "Can't Let Go." As I've mentioned I often use my falsetto to sing, including the high notes of the divas, Tichina didn't know. I hear her saying, "Who is that? She's good!" Well, it was me and I'm not a she. But I give Mariah a run for her money, our faithful's say.

All-Star Karaoke has become a destination for many of my favorite vocalists. And as powerful as their voices are, they also come to play. When R&B diva Alyson Williams comes by, she'll do her song, "Just Call My Name" or "Alfie" by Dionne Warwick. But then she'll join me on Natalie Cole's, "Our Love."

Monifah is a vocalist I've appreciated since Heavy D brought her onto the scene in the late '90s. She was that perfect blend of great singer and what was happening in the hip-hop swing of music at the time. Her big hits, "Home" and "Touch It," flew to the top of the charts. Heavy D treated her as Berry Gordy treated Diana Ross. But her ride to sustain recording industry success would be short-lived and she and Heavy D would part ways. Through some difficult times, including a run with drugs, Monifah seems to have reentered the world and the industry through a courageous film of authenticity. She's now living her life out and proud, has a gorgeous wife named Terez, is a mother and a grandmother, and is an independent artist who is often booked. She and I share stages inside programming for the black and LGBTQ communities. Having come by our Native spot, Monifah was the first singer of note to walk into All-Star Karaoke at Billie's Black on Tuesday nights. She sang Jill Scott's, "The Way" and Bonnie Raitt's, "Let's Give Them Something to Talk About." She and I cut the fool on the Emotions, "Best of My Love." She and Terez often come and ask for me to sing from on high tracks like Maxwell's,

"This Woman's Work" and Earth, Wind & Fire's "Reasons," showcasing Phillip Bailey's ultimate falsetto.

In April 2014, my dear friend, industry publicist Gwendolyn Quinn said All-Star Karaoke is the first place her newly-signed client should go to get some buzz on her new single and to experience a cool room of people and performances. To hear her describe it like that meant so much to me. When KeKe arrived, her team said she'd only do her song, but would eat and enjoy the evening as others were in cue to karaoke. And when I tell you she sang her song plus she had the track for a cover record by Patti LaBelle she'd recorded several years back, she also did, "If Only You Knew." But when Ant asked me to serenade him something for his birthday, his request wasn't a love song, but Whitney Houston's, "I Wanna Dance With Somebody." I acquiesced as that's one of his favorites to hear me sing when we do one-on-one karaoke in the Korea town where they have private suites. In an out-of-body moment, KeKe was feeling the spirit and the next thing you know she's hopped on the stage, got the other mic and she and I are singing together. It was a total rush and another video that whenever it posts, gets lots of love.

Another time, I recall my brother talking about seeing some of my karaoke clips on YouTube and that he enjoyed them. He continued. "I saw your Earth, Wind, & Fire's "Reasons" and Maxwell's "This Woman's Work. And your Michael Jackson, "Love Never Felt Like This." "Good job," he offered.

But as proof that homophobia lives, he said, "I skipped your, "All The Man I Need." "It wasn't for you," I retorted. "It was for Ant."

That memory gives me a giggle because it underscores how long it had been since that shaming feeling around my orientation and my love of singing women's songs had been a factor. Certainly, there was residue there. But had I not shut out the array of homophobic daggers that have come my way since childhood, I just might not have hit this place of liberation and joy around my singing and even karaoke, now called by Airbnb, one of the best NYC karaoke experiences around.

Had I listened, I might not have landed Ant, who has unflinchingly encouraged me to audition for shows and pursue my passions.

Though I never wanted to pursue it professionally, singing is important to me. And I think we should always use and take care of our instruments. I consider it a blessing that I found karaoke as an outlet for that piece of me that enjoys vocalizing and a good olé' sing along. So, for me, I want to cheer those ladies on who do it professionally and well. They entertain me. And if from time to time, they'll pop by and sing a ditty with me for five minutes or less, my living and love for them will not be in vain.

SCRAPBOOK

We too had a fabulous all-star appearance during Motown May 2014, Xosha Roquemore!

Laurieann Gibson is the go-to choreographer and creative director for the best in the businesslike Lady Gaga, Katy Perry, Nicki Minaj and more. Her vision propels the careers of performers. Her working, and always impressive, client list also includes Sean "Puffy" Combs, Fantasia Barrino, Tamar Braxton, French Montana and many more

I know Shiba Russell for the many years she worked as an anchor in New York City at the NBC affiliate. She's currently in the NBC family still but also works for WXIA in Atlanta as an anchor for its morning news show.

This is at Billie's Black presents All-Star Karaoke with Patrick L. Riley May 2014.

Marva Hicks—'Gladys Knight' in Motown the Musical on Broadway—came to All-Star Karaoke to choose our Motown May winner. It was like American Idol that night in May 2014.

I usually see Marva Hicks at Broadway events in New York, but ran into her in October 2009, in Los Angeles at the Sherman Oaks estate of Oz Scott, the renowned director and producer.

Marva Hicks played Gladys Knight in the first run of Motown the Musical on Broadway. Here we are at a preview of the show on September 27, 2012.

Mica Hughes is a University of Maryland College Park communications graduate who has reported. But modeling has been her strong suit. She is a top model with Wilhelmina Models and Ford Models. Mica has done the catwalk for all the majors including Oscar de la Renta, Yves Saint Laurent and Chanel. Now, she services models who are trying to break in via her modeling agency, Mica Models. Mica is an entrepreneur of note, a karaoke enthusiast and a Harlem resident.

Mica Hughes came to my All-Star Karaoke events well before she was cast on Bravo TV's **Blood, Sweat, & Heels**. Here we are at Billie's Black Spring 2013. We could always count on Mica lighting up the room.

Kimberly Nichole is a Spelman graduate, the first college-educated member of her family back in Seattle. She started her career utilizing her economics degree in a fashion industry human resources job. Then, the open mic scene in New York swept her back to center and her passion which was to sing, "very edgy, blues, rock and roll." And she typically brings a rock ballerina aesthetic to her stages including an EP in the marketplace called **Rock Ballerina: tutus**. She was also on **The Voice** and fared well. She has a 9-track album titled, **Yellow Brick Journey** that she recorded in 2010. She reloaded it as an EP in 2012.

Kimberly Nichole came by All-Star Karaoke to sing with us! Spring 2016:

Kimberly Nichole at an East Side NYC event that our girlfriend Sidra Smith put on for Sphatika Spa July 2015.

Russell Simmons' label Def Jam signed Alyson Williams to its label in the late '80s. The debut Def Jam album, **Raw**, was a hit including the mega-hit from 1990-01 that stayed on the charts for 67 weeks. She continues to bring her R&B and jazz style all around New York and New Jersey as well as all over the globe.

Alyson Williams at All-Star Karaoke December 2015. Billie's Black.

It was 1990 when Keke Wyatt first came on the scene. But she made a splash in 2001 with her debut album **Soul Sista**. She has one of the most belting yet precise voices in the industry. America got to know her zany personality on the docu-series, **R&B Divas** which chronicled the women of soul who are still making it happen in the business. She quickly became a fan favorite as a singer and as a reality show character. Some of her other albums include, **Rated Love**, **Keke Covers**, and **Country Fried Soul**.

Singer Keke Wyatt came by All-Star Karaoke and sang Whitney's "I Wanna Dance with Somebody" with me! We had a blast! April 2014. Billie's Black Restaurant. Harlem, NY.

ALL-STAR KARAOKE | 313

Monifah was raised in the East Harlem section of New York City. America got reacquainted with Monifah who resurfaced – with her wife Terez in tow. As an out and proud performer, more fans get to benefit from her new releases and steady performance schedule.

Acknowledgements

So many women who inspired, and continue to inspire me, aren't all referenced in the anecdotal prose that makes up these heartfelt chapters. Therefore, I use this acknowledgement section to attempt to name many more knowing that the list is even longer than my brain's attempt at this current list.

Of course, my mother Queen Elizabeth Bellinger Riley is a highlight in this time. She was my first diva. I'm forever grateful to her and forever grieving without her. I'm Happy I could take a little time to reflect on that era in my life before the pain from her passing. We did have 23 years of mostly joy that we got to experience together inside her lifetime. It must count as a blessing.

At the same time, I have to shout out mom's mother, Saphronia Haynes Bellinger, and my dad's mom, Daisy Mae Wallace Riley, as well as my maternal Grand Aunts Baby, Tuga, and Lilla, and my mom's sister, the ever-devoted Aunt Mary Lee. My Dad's sisters Charlie Mae, Dorothy, and my favorite Aunt Goldie are also among the stalwart supporters of me throughout my life. These are women whose magic I have experienced first-hand. On that same frequency, I acknowledge a couple of special, maternal cousins who translate as "other" mothers, Mamie Prescott and Rosa Mae Brown.

If mom was my first diva, my sister Janice was reluctantly my second. Thanks for your love, Janice.

Like siblings, I have an illuminating array of extended family members who've been an inspirational difference to me including a half dozen or so of my sister's own best girlfriends who've become much like my own big sisters including Lisa Smith, Terri Steele Morton, Ruby Cummings, Stephanie Maxwell, Jacqualine Dixon, Cassandra Railey, Renee "Pepper" Long, Aquilla McIntosh, Teresa Horne Ayers and Kaye Burwell. My familial muses include cousins Harriet Gray, Felecia Cuthpert, Kejuanna Manor, Sylathea Prescott Hutchins and so many more.

My siblings and my upbringing as Air Force brats means we bonded with other families wherever we traveled. The matriarch of the Bethea family, Christine Ellerbee Bethea, was a constant presence for us through all of our lives, from Tokyo to Georgia to California and back to Georgia through my adult years. And there were several other special women whose names deserve placement as influences including Evangeline Henson, Susie Evans, Maurena Maynor and my potty trainer Miss Gessie Jeter, a neighbor in Valdosta, Ga.

My teachers and professors have always been special to me and I could go on and on about them all. But a couple who stand out as personal inspirations are Mrs. Linda Green from my time at Windsor Forest High School in Savannah, Georgia and Dr. Ann Kimbrough, from Clark Atlanta University. They gave me hands-on love and have yet to let me go. With social media, I feel the continued care and compassion of my many amazing educators through the years, and I love you all for believing in me and letting me know today that I've done okay for myself. I continue to wish each of you well.

In my business, women were always at the center of my mentoring including Monica Kaufman (Pearson), Sidmel Estes-Sumpter, Amanda Davis, Brenda Wood, Sheila Stainback, Robin Stone, Katti Gray, Paula Madison, Oprah Winfrey, Gayle King, Barbara Ciara, Sheila Brooks, Condace Pressley, Angela Robinson, Gwen Rouse, Eloise Dudley, Lucy Galliher, Wanda M. Akin, Terrie Williams, Harriette Cole, Dr. Anne Watts, Xernona Clayton, Jamie Foster Brown, Cynthia Horner, and many more.

Alongside me on the inspiration train have always been amazing ladies in my life including high school BFF Natalie Palmer, Rachel Allen, Lori Jones Lewis, Latecia Engram, Bernadette Young, Tonja

Denmark Prince, Yvette Jones, Tandi Reddick, Felecia Roberts, Sam Maynor Walker, Itika Oldwine, Jakki Taylor Richardson, Lesia Minor, Candi Carter, Sherry Champion, Sally Lou Loveman, Audrey Irvine, Adrianne C. Smith, Faedra Chatard, Cassi Davis, Sharon Epperson, Lisa Bryan, Berlinda Garnett, Rita Thompson, Patrice Graves, Carla Jackson, Nichole Andrews, Sidra Smith, Sabrina Coleman, Penwah, Chanel Harper, Brina Milton, Manivone Clayton, Dawn Murphy Riley, Mara Schiavocampo, Tawana Matthews, Paula Witt, Adrene Clarke Williams, Rhonda Ross, Lisa Goodnight, Michelle Hord, Dawn Kelly, Rachelle Weston, Elise Durham, Kelly Welborn, Miko Branch, Bernice Wooden, Yvette Noel-Schure, Rachelle Weston, Patti Webster, Terrie Williams, L. Marilyn Crawford, Dorinda Walker, Robin Lynn, Sharon Nelson, Antoinette White, Michelle Sanchez-Boyce, Cynthia Burgos, Chandra Jones, Berlinda Garnett, Camille Morrison, Cindy Phillips Baumgartner, Chandra Thomas Whitfield, Chloe Hilliard, Stephanie Elam, Terri Prettyman Bowles, Ava Duvernay, Kaye Burwell, Dr. Joan Lewis, Carol Mitchell-Leon, Theresa Minor, Tanika Ray, Shaun Robinson, Tiffany Zeno, Bevy Smith, Michaela angela Davis, Adriane Ferguson, Angelique Frances, Robyn Greene Arrington, Victoria McGinnis, Jennifer Bisram, Shareen King, Evolyn Brooks Mack, Michele Baldwin, Roxanne Jones, Lesley Pitts, Adrianne C. Smith, Bernice Wooden, Jacque Reid, Grace Kisa, Jocelyn Coleman, Eugenia Harvey, Lola Ogunnaike, Sharon Carpenter, Kai Brown, Blair Younger, Joicelyn Dingle, Kierna Mayo, Tonya Giddens, Mara Brock-Akil, Dorothy Williams, Yannick Rice Lamb, Ingrid Sturgis, Bonnie Newman Davis, Cheryl Smith, Sarah Glover, Kirsten Poe Hill, journalist Vanessa Williams, Callie Crossley, Sandra Bookman, Doreen Oliver, Monique Oliver, Nekesa Moody, Alicia Quarles, Dorothy Butler Gilliam, Kathy Times, Angelique Francis, Tagan Lee, Janelle Richards, Rowena Husbands, Francina Jewel Blake, Ruth Priester, Jackie Bazan, Evelyn Santana, Sheila Eldridge, Tonya Giddens, Dr. Wanda Brockington, Carol Johnson Green, Denise Clay, Malena Cunningham, Angelique McFarland, Melora Rivera, Kiki Williams, Constance White, Beverly Bond,

Tonya Giddens, Yvette Hayward, Sharon Quinn, Marion Boullon, Charlie T, Danielle Johnson, Adriane Ferguson and Charon Richardson, to name just a few.

Of course, many men inspire me, but sticking to the theme, I'll name a few who know what this project means to me. My dad, Retired CMSGT Herman L. Riley has always been a support of what comes out of my unique lens. Dad's wife, Diana, has, in turn, become a loving and appreciated booster of my passions for the past twenty years. My brother Herman may not have always embraced it early on but has grown to accept me as his not-straight-identified, women-loving brother. His son, Herman, is my only sibling offspring who carries his own flicker of light and enthusiasm for his favorite female singers and celebs. Like his proud, impressionable uncle. And of course, there are my male cousins of honorable note: Judge Clarence "Tabby" Cuthpert, Eric Prescott and Elliott Buddah Gray among a host of many other great, loyal and loving guys from my family.

My male influences and BFFs over the years have also inspired, and continue to inspire, me - palpably inside all of the passing seasons of my life. These include Nene Ofuatey Kodjoe, Jimmy Bethea, Maurice Tony Evans, Ernest Maynor, Creswell Formey, Kevin Williams, Dr. Reginald Parker, Maurice Marable, Derrick Hemphill, Reinaldo Cummings Jr., Nigel Nanton, Michael K. Watts, James Coaxum, Eddie Reynolds, Devon Settles, Lajuan Meyer, Lee Smith, Carl Nelson, Ryan Williams, Brian Henderson, Caleb Wilkerson, Theo Perry, Frankie Edozien, Gil Robertson, Musa Jackson, Warren Bell, Curtis Dennis, Dustin Fitzharris, Demarcio Slaughter, Wade Hanley, Marlon Layne, Howard Chisholm, Kendrick Reid, Keyon Williams, RJ Beale, Robert Vickers, Vic Carter, Mike Woolfolk, Glenn Proctor, Glenn Tunstall, Leo Preziosi, Glenn Rice, Will Sutton, Tom Morgan, Herb Lowe, Jason Johnson, Stan Chambers, Jr., Merrell Hollis, David Nathan, Nick Tedd, Sean Lyons, Harris Bostic, Dan Gunn, Fred Rimando, Drew Berry, Jinah Miranda Houston, Scott Coleman, Scott Hamilton, Stacey Antonio, Derek Lafayette, Ed Roebuck, Terrence Johnson, Marlon Millner, Lloyd Boston, Darius Booker, Ray

Dotch, Kevin Anthony, Sean Hollingsworth, Roy Johnson, Jamar Dunn, Ryan Taliafaro Hall, Lamoh Hicks, Kenny Miles, Jason Frazer, Bobby Towns, Tony Phillips, Ken Rye, Darris Henson, Tom Morgan, Vincent Priester, Floyd Grant, Clay Cane, Charlie Lewis, Kenneth Miles, Mashaun Simon, Geraldo Rivera, Al Roker, Gregory Douglas, Marcellous Jones, Mario Ephriam, Anthony Preston, Kiwan Anderson, Derek Lafayette, Keith Wooten, Wardell Malloy, Kofi Bannerman, Dr. Ian Smith, Darius Brown, George Faison, Tad Schnugg, Nick Ashford, Marc Sir Dane, Lex Sturdivant, Dwayne Palmer, Bill Nunn, Monty Ross, Herbert Eichelberger, Kenny Leon, Spike Lee, Donald Bogle, David Nathan, Craig Seymour, Rev. Raphael Warnock, Gerald Boyd, Roy Hobbs, Zachry Boyd, Terrance Russ, Rodney Pope, Michael Bryant, Winfield Johnston, Jay Davis, Doug Weathers, Clarence Williams, Bobby Roache, James Dubose, Kenneth Carr, Dr. Russ Robinson, James Francis, Gregory Dunmore, Eddie Harris, Shaquille O'Neal, Karu Daniels, Lawrence Floyd, Lamoh HIcks, Derek J, Michael Baumgartner, Emil Wilbekin, Devon Johnson, Ronnie Wright, David Bridgeforth, Waddie Grant, Darius Walker, B.D. Heath, Jonathan Roper, Terry Allen, Donald Bogle, Tavis Smiley, Ben McLaurin, Arthur Fennell, Greg Coy, Kevin Powell, Keith Carl Howard, Terrence Johnson, Marlon Millner, Terrance Russ, Reggie Van Lee, and The Game who once told me he was a fan of my blog. I can't make this stuff up.

Thanks to the best man in my life, Anthony Harper, for always pushing me to be my personal and creative best. You have a front row seat to seeing me juggle ownership of my corner of the sky among the galaxy of my favorite female stars. It can be dwarfing sometimes, but you always show up as my #1 fan when I need you to. And you know I'm your #1 fan. A special shout out to Ant's mom, Jacqui Washington Harper with whom I share a life-long adoration for Ant – and Miss Diana Ross whose sold-out show we got to enjoy together recently at the Denver Opera House.

This project would not be without my publishing inspirations, some of whom date back a decade or so ago when I originally tried to get a book published, including Janet Hill Talbert, Gilda Squire, Terrance Dean, Melonyce Mcafee, Tracy Sherrod and Robert Guinsler. To my editor Clarence Haynes, I'm eternally grateful that you challenged me to reflect, write and share vulnerably and with authenticity, which made this process challenging, therapeutic and healing. I knew you were the one to get me there and we did it, together. Thank you. Excelsior.

And the woman who inspired me to do this project, Dorpie Books Publisher Yolanda Young. Thank you. We met many years ago and have continued to network and engage via the National Association of Black Journalists. You've always been able to call on me to present or host an event for you, always welcomed synergies. Your belief in me on this project came in the nick of time, and I'm forever appreciative that you had me on your heart to help launch your publishing house. My honor to serve as a mascot of possibilities in publishing for my fellow media professionals out there who know they have a book in them.

And to those un-named and un-sung, please charge it to my overwhelmed head and not my eternally grateful heart. I am so clear that I am not here on my own. And I know I stand on the shoulders, and shoulder pads, of a world community of uplifting forces. I thank each and every one of you who have been a forwarding part of this journey. I am so humbled.